They Want Your Money and Your Life.

Truths you must know about the coming depression, economic war and years of crisis.

Vernon Coleman

Vernon Coleman: What the papers say:

'By the year 2020 there will be a holocaust, not caused by a plutonium plume but by greed, medical ambition and political opportunism. This is the latest vision of Vernon Coleman, an articulate and prolific medical author…this disturbing book detects diseases in the whole way we deliver health care.' – Sunday Times (1988)

'…the issues explores he explores are central to the health of the nation.' – Nursing Times

'It is not necessary to accept his conclusion to be able to savour his decidedly trenchant comments on today's medicine…a book to stimulate and to make one argue.' – British Medical Journal

'As a writer of medical bestsellers, Dr Vernon Coleman's aim is to shock us out of our complacency…it's impossible not to be impressed by some of his arguments.' – Western Daily Press

'Controversial and devastating' – Publishing News

'Dr Coleman produces mountains of evidence to justify his outrageous claims.' – Edinburgh Evening News

'Dr Coleman lays about him with an uncompromising verbal scalpel, dipped in vitriol, against all sorts of sacred medical cows.' – Exeter Express and Echo

'Vernon Coleman writes brilliant books.' – The Good Book Guide

'No thinking person can ignore him. This is why he has been for over 20 years one of the world's leading advocates on human and animal rights in relation to health. Long may it continue.' – The Ecologist

'The calmest voice of reason comes from Dr Vernon Coleman.' – The Observer

'A godsend.' – Daily Telegraph

'Dr Vernon Coleman has justifiably acquired a reputation for being controversial, iconoclastic and influential.' – General Practitioner

'Superstar.' – Independent on Sunday

'Brilliant!' – The People

'Compulsive reading.' – The Guardian

'He is certainly someone whose views are impossible to ignore, with his passionate advocacy of human and animal rights.' – International Journal of Alternative and Complementary Medicine
'The doctor who dares to speak his mind.' – Oxford Mail
'Dr Coleman speaks openly and reassuringly.' – Oxford Times
'He writes lucidly and wittily.' – Good Housekeeping

Books by Vernon Coleman include:

Medical
The Medicine Men
Paper Doctors
Everything You Want To Know About Ageing
The Home Pharmacy
Aspirin or Ambulance
Face Values
Stress and Your Stomach
A Guide to Child Health
Guilt
The Good Medicine Guide
An A to Z of Women's Problems
Bodypower
Bodysense
Taking Care of Your Skin
Life without Tranquillisers
High Blood Pressure
Diabetes
Arthritis
Eczema and Dermatitis
The Story of Medicine
Natural Pain Control
Mindpower
Addicts and Addictions
Dr Vernon Coleman's Guide to Alternative Medicine
Stress Management Techniques
Overcoming Stress
The Health Scandal
The 20 Minute Health Check
Sex for Everyone
Mind over Body
Eat Green Lose Weight
Why Doctors Do More Harm Than Good
The Drugs Myth

Complete Guide to Sex
How to Conquer Backache
How to Conquer Pain
Betrayal of Trust
Know Your Drugs
Food for Thought
The Traditional Home Doctor
Relief from IBS
The Parent's Handbook
Men in Bras, Panties and Dresses
Power over Cancer
How to Conquer Arthritis
How to Stop Your Doctor Killing You
Superbody
Stomach Problems – Relief at Last
How to Overcome Guilt
How to Live Longer
Coleman's Laws
Millions of Alzheimer Patients Have Been Misdiagnosed
Climbing Trees at 112
Is Your Health Written in the Stars?
The Kick-Ass A–Z for over 60s
Briefs Encounter
The Benzos Story
Dementia Myth
Waiting

Psychology/Sociology
Stress Control
How to Overcome Toxic Stress
Know Yourself (1988)
Stress and Relaxation
People Watching
Spiritpower
Toxic Stress
I Hope Your Penis Shrivels Up
Oral Sex: Bad Taste and Hard To Swallow
Other People's Problems

The 100 Sexiest, Craziest, Most Outrageous Agony Column
Questions (and Answers) Of All Time
How to Relax and Overcome Stress
Too Sexy To Print
Psychiatry
Are You Living With a Psychopath?

Politics and General
England Our England
Rogue Nation
Confronting the Global Bully
Saving England
Why Everything Is Going To Get Worse Before It Gets Better
The Truth They Won't Tell You...About The EU
Living In a Fascist Country
How to Protect & Preserve Your Freedom, Identity & Privacy
Oil Apocalypse
Gordon is a Moron
The OFPIS File
What Happens Next?
Bloodless Revolution
2020
Stuffed
The Shocking History of the EU
Coming Apocalypse
Covid-19: The Greatest Hoax in History
Old Man in a Chair
Endgame
Proof that Masks do more Harm than Good
Covid-19: The Fraud Continues
Covid-19: Exposing the Lies
Social Credit: Nightmare on Your Street
NHS: What's wrong and how to put it right

Diaries and Autobiographies
Diary of a Disgruntled Man
Just another Bloody Year
Bugger off and Leave Me Alone

Return of the Disgruntled Man
Life on the Edge
The Game's Afoot
Tickety Tonk
Memories 1
Memories 2
My Favourite Books

Animals
Why Animal Experiments Must Stop
Fighting For Animals
Alice and Other Friends
Animal Rights – Human Wrongs
Animal Experiments – Simple Truths

General Non Fiction
How to Publish Your Own Book
How to Make Money While Watching TV
Strange but True
Daily Inspirations
Why Is Public Hair Curly
People Push Bottles Up Peaceniks
Secrets of Paris
Moneypower
101 Things I Have Learned
100 Greatest Englishmen and Englishwomen
Cheese Rolling, Shin Kicking and Ugly Tattoos
One Thing after Another

Novels (General)
Mrs Caldicot's Cabbage War
Mrs Caldicot's Knickerbocker Glory
Mrs Caldicot's Oyster Parade
Mrs Caldicot's Turkish Delight
Deadline
Second Chance
Tunnel
Mr Henry Mulligan

The Truth Kills
Revolt
My Secret Years with Elvis
Balancing the Books
Doctor in Paris
Stories with a Twist in the Tale (short stories)
Dr Bullock's Annals

The Young Country Doctor Series
Bilbury Chronicles
Bilbury Grange
Bilbury Revels
Bilbury Country
Bilbury Village
Bilbury Pie (short stories)
Bilbury Pudding (short stories)
Bilbury Tonic
Bilbury Relish
Bilbury Mixture
Bilbury Delights
Bilbury Joys
Bilbury Tales
Bilbury Days
Bilbury Memories

Novels (Sport)
Thomas Winsden's Cricketing Almanack
Diary of a Cricket Lover
The Village Cricket Tour
The Man Who Inherited a Golf Course
Around the Wicket
Too Many Clubs and Not Enough Balls

Cat books
Alice's Diary
Alice's Adventures
We Love Cats
Cats Own Annual

The Secret Lives of Cats
Cat Basket
The Cataholics' Handbook
Cat Fables
Cat Tales
Catoons from Catland

As Edward Vernon
Practice Makes Perfect
Practise What You Preach
Getting Into Practice
Aphrodisiacs – An Owner's Manual
The Complete Guide to Life

Written with Donna Antoinette Coleman
How to Conquer Health Problems between Ages 50 & 120
Health Secrets Doctors Share With Their Families
Animal Miscellany
England's Glory
Wisdom of Animals

Legal Disclaimer

Although this book contains my views on a number of issues
(including finance) I am not an accredited investment adviser and
nor am I a professional financial adviser. Nothing in this book
should be regarded as personal investment advice.

Note from the author

Please note that I do not have any social media accounts. All
accounts which appear to be in my name are fake. I have been
banned by YouTube, Facebook, LinkedIn and so on. Accounts in my
name on Twitter and Telegram and all other social media platforms
are nothing to do with me and should be labelled as fake however
real they may appear. The only sites where my work appears and
which I control are www.vernoncoleman.com and
www.vernoncoleman.org – though I have always allowed my videos
to be reproduced on other sites as long as they are not cut or edited
or adorned with advertisements.

Dedication

To Antoinette, as always.

You are the reason my heart beats and I know that will never change. Your courage, determination and skill have helped save the lives of thousands and have opened the minds of millions more.

Introduction

If we are to survive the future, and the inevitable global financial crash, we need to understand the past. My very real fear is that we are heading for the worse depression in history. And it is going to be permanent.

There are, I fear, many millions of people who still think that everything that is happening in the world is just bad luck. On December 28 2022, a *Country Life* editorial talked of 'making sense in an increasingly irrational world'.

And a magazine called *Investors' Chronicle* described 2022 as 'a year of shocks'.

Oh dear.

Sadly, the writers of those editorials were not alone.

The majority of people still believe that their government wants to help them (when government ministers have shown that they are solely interested in power and money), that financial institutions are honest and well-meaning (when their sole aim is to make money at any cost, without any concern for the traditional widows and orphans) that drug companies are full of fine people fighting illness (when drug companies can easily be proved to be the most corrupt, dishonest and wicked companies on earth, and the people who work for them are exclusively venal and uncaring). And exceptionally naive commentators in the media seem convinced that everything will soon go back to normal, when all the signs show very clearly that unless we stand up and speak out things will never go back to what most people still think of as 'normal'.

If only the only problem was that the world was irrational and that commentators were too blind to see what has happened and what is going to happen next.

In this book I intend to show that the truth is that the world is very rational indeed. Everything that is happening is happening with a purpose. All our institutions have not just failed us – as many people feel they have. On the contrary they have actively, deliberately betrayed us. The global economic outlook is more uncertain today than it has been since World War II, and mainstream forecasters are underestimating the severity of the problems which will become apparent over the next year or two. The coming problems will be systemic and permanent and not transient. Nothing is happening by accident. Can anyone really believe that health services have been destroyed and that the global economy has crashed because of a well-marketed but no more than usually dangerous brand of the annual flu?

The alternative explanation is that all medical advisers around the world made exactly the same mistakes at the same time and that all central banks also made exactly the same mistakes at the same time. No rational being can possibly be so besotted by affection for coincidence that they would believe such nonsense.

For the record, I predicted just about everything that happened in 2022 at least one and sometimes two years earlier. There were no big surprises. Long before they happened, I forecast high inflation, rising interest rates, falling growth and productivity and rapidly increasing energy and food prices. I warned about the side effects with the covid-19 jabs in 2020, and in the early spring of that year I warned that governments were using a fake pandemic to introduce compulsory vaccines, to kill the elderly and to get rid of cash. It wasn't difficult to make these predictions because everything that is happening has been planned. Once you understand how evil the conspirators really are (and what their aims are) it isn't difficult to see what they intend to do next.

I know some readers will probably think that all this makes me sound like a lunatic. But, in the true tradition of baddies such as Ernst Stavro Blofeld, the conspirators really do want to take over the world. It's all about power and money. The conspirators want all the remaining oil for themselves. They know it's running out and they want to keep their obscene super-yachts moving. They also want enough fuel for planes and for bombing foreigners.

To those who smirk and snigger I would point out that everything I have warned about over the last few years has been proved to be accurate.

The intelligent observer only needs to look around to see the signs.

The oil shortage is now eternal and getting worse. Extra taxes on oil companies mean that exploration is halting. Banks won't support companies which are looking for more oil. The EU's policies on tankers, and their insurance, means that the worldwide flow of oil will be hampered and that prices are bound to rise further. The EU, remember, was always the conspirators' first step towards an unelected, brutal world government. Those who support the EU are collaborators of the very worst kind.

As Russian oil disappears from the market the other producers will have ever more power. The price of oil is just going to go up.

Hypocrisies and closed minds are everywhere.

Race campaigners (inspired, cheered on and paid to protest) will take down a statue or protest about some vague perceived slight, but I haven't seen them complaining about the hundreds of millions who are starving to death in Africa and Asia because of massively high food and fuel prices.

Europe, while pretending to be very green and committed to net zero, is importing huge quantities of chopped up trees to burn to make electricity, and being supplied with liquefied natural gas which is imported from the United States in huge diesel powered tankers. Within Europe, 573 billion euros of taxpayers' money has been spent on keeping energy prices affordable. That sort of money isn't available in Africa or Asia.

The next problem for Europe is that the gas storage tanks were filled with Russian gas long ago. That isn't going to happen before next winter. Moreover, Chinese imports of LNG gas were low because of China's crazy zero covid policies. When those end the Chinese will be buying up all the gas. If you think the winter of 2022/23 was bad for prices, and feeling cold, just wait until next winter.

Digitalisation, compulsory vaccination and a global social credit programme are part of the plan to control everything we do. The enemy will keep the fear levels as high as they can with starvation, economic collapse, wars and endless threats of new diseases. And, of course, vaccine injury deaths are classified as 'sudden adult death syndrome'. They'll never blame the vaccines for anything.

Soon, they'll link the vaccines to the digitalisation and you won't be able to do anything if you haven't had all the required compulsory jabs. I warned about that years ago, as regular readers will remember.

And now they're giving the useless and toxic covid-19 jab to infants.

They're going to add a jab that doesn't work and isn't safe to an aggressive, untested, officially promoted programme of mass medication; the most alarming, experimental and grandiose example of centrally approved child abuse in human history; a programme that I believe has done infinitely more harm than good; a drug administration mania that should have been halted decades ago by the medical profession, and would have been if the medical profession hadn't been bought by the drug industry; an untested experimental schedule that would have warmed the evil heart of Josef Mengele.

There are so many unanswered questions. The questions are unanswered because officially they have never been asked.

For example, is it more dangerous to give the mRNA jab to babies whose mothers were jabbed before or during pregnancy? No one knows.

In America, the Government recommends that babies and infants should be given the following vaccines before they are 15 months old: three doses for hepatitis B, two doses for rotavirus, four doses for diphtheria, tetanus and pertussis, four doses for haemophilus influenza, four doses of pneumococcal conjugate, three doses for polio, another one for influenza, one for measles, mumps and rubella, one for varicella, one for hepatitis and so on and so on…the list never ends.

And now they've added in the toxic covid-19 jab. Why they don't just slaughter infants at birth is a mystery. After 18 months they receive endless armfuls of more stuff. How kids ever get time to go to school is a mystery. And, of course, it's all much the same the world over.

How much testing has been done to check that all these vaccines don't interact badly in the developing human body? None would be a good answer. How much research is done to see how much damage is being done to the developing immune system? Again, try none as your answer. Nearly all the medical research done these days is done by drug companies. Why would they want to find out how much damage their junk is doing?

And doctors seem astonished and bewildered by the fact that autism, ADHD, allergies, asthma and probably every disease beginning with A are all getting commoner every year. Just a coincidence, they say. Better diagnoses, they say. It never occurs to

4

Researchers keep producing evidence to show that unvaccinated Americans are healthier than vaccinated Americans and that scheduled vaccines cause much chronic illness. A large number of illnesses, including infections, allergies and behavioural issues are commoner among children who'd received a number of vaccinations. Doctors who speak or write about this in public lose their licence to practice. That is now standard practice and it is one of the reasons few doctors dare speak out.

There is tons of evidence – much of which I quoted in my book on vaccination called *Anyone who tells you vaccines are safe and effective is lying* – which questions the validity of vaccination programmes.

But all debate is silenced. The science about vaccination, like some guilty family secret, has been locked away and must never be discussed.

And now the covid-19 jab is going to be part of that massive routine vaccination programme for infants.

We are at the beginning of what will, I fear, be the longest, darkest financial depression in history. Households have already suffered the biggest drop in real incomes since records began in the 1950s. And things are going to get much worse. Investment predictions are being made by commentators who still believe that accidents and coincidences drove us into the current situation. Bankers and financial journalists may sneer and insist that the current recession will be over in a few months, that inflation will be back under 2% before anyone can blink and that everything will shortly be back to what we have been led to believe was 'normal' but I can see no evidence to support those optimistic views though that was exactly what they were saying at the start of 2023.

I don't believe them and their reassurances seem to me to be just another part of the plot to confuse and to create despair.

Historically, once inflation goes above 8% it usually takes a decade to get back down to what used to be regarded as normal. Today, things are very different because the inflation we see now has been created quite deliberately. Only a very deep and lasting depression will bring down inflation. When prices rise dramatically they don't go back to where they were – and they usually keep rising for several years. And it's vital to remember that the only way for governments to pay off their obscene levels of debt is to continue to force up inflation. And although the interest on the UK Government's debts will cost taxpayers hundreds of billions (and that's without paying off the capital) the Bank of England won't dare put up interest rates enough to conquer inflation because of the danger of a very major, and politically unacceptable, house price crash.

Huge amounts of taxpayers' money is being used to pay the cost of quantitative easing. The total owed is so great that if you have children then their children's children's children will still be paying off the debts the Government has accumulated in the last three years. Our collective legacy will be debt. That's the way they want it.

Remember: you (and your children, and their children) will own nothing.

The unavoidable truth is that everything we used to value has been devalued. You'd have to be blind not to see the pattern. The quality of health care has deteriorated beyond recognition and in Britain it is clear that the health care available today (both inside and outside hospitals) is significantly poorer than it was over half a century ago.

The law is not now about justice, it is about power – obtaining and maintaining power by any means possible.

The media is not about sharing news, comment or advice – it is exclusively about power and money. (Any journalist who uses the word 'pandemic' without the word 'fake' in front of it is either ignorant or crooked.)

The trade unions do not exist to look after their members – they exist to use their power in the service of the conspirators.

This book is concerned with the way the conspirators have deliberately destroyed the global economy in order to achieve their aims of banishing cash, creating a digital society, creating an environment in which billions will die (initially in Africa and Asia), promoting the system of living based on social credit and fulfilling their aim of creating a world in which the vast majority will (in their words) 'own nothing and be happy'. It is about the ways in which those aims are being achieved and about the ways in which our society is being destroyed in the name of the fake cult of 'climate change'.

Everything is designed to weaken, to destroy and impoverish. Whenever anything strange and seemingly inexplicable occurs we simply have to ask ourselves: 'How does this help the conspirators? How does this move us towards a digital world, the Great Reset and a world in which we own nothing?'

Nothing that has happened in the last three years (from 2020 onwards) has ever happened before and yet, as the months have passed by, very little that has happened has been a surprise. Interest rates are the lowest they have been for 5,000 years which is another way of saying 'ever'. Governments around the world have borrowed more money, and acquired more debt, than ever before. Central banks have created more money than ever before. Governments have acted in unison in a way never seen before. Bankers and investors lent money to riskier and riskier companies – with unprecedented enthusiasm – as they struggled to make money in an era where zero interest rates were considered generous. Interest rates were kept extremely low (to the huge benefit of young house buyers and property developers) for longer than at any time in history. Governments and banks actually started selling bonds with negative interest rates – requiring those buying the bonds to pay money for the privilege of owning the bonds. Nothing like this had ever happened before. For the first time in history, seemingly intelligent people started to put all their money into crypto-currencies which were promoted with wild enthusiasm by celebrities and which existed only on someone's computer. (One unfortunate investor accidentally threw away a hard drive containing a fortune and has spent years hoping to find it.) Everything became a bubble. Classic cars were sold at such astronomical prices that they were too valuable to drive and became art exhibits. Collectors began buying art work which you couldn't hold or hang on your wall and which existed only in a computer. Global lockdowns were introduced for no reason and for the first time in history. An infection which the UK Government's own advisors accepted was no worse than the annual flu was announced to be some sort of new plague – something that had never happened before. The words 'pandemic' and 'plague' were used by journalists who clearly had no idea what either word really meant. Citizens were told to stay away from work and were given huge amounts of taxpayers' money while they stayed at home watching television. This had never happened before. Schools were closed for absolutely no good reason. Doctors and hospitals introduced an entirely worthless and potentially dangerous test which became legally required. And a new form of vaccine was introduced, which did not do what it was said to do, was far more dangerous than the authorities admitted and had not been properly tested, and was then given to billions of people around the world. Celebrities of various sorts all promoted the new vaccine even though I suspect that none of them understood what they were promoting. Doctors and nurses then gave billions of doses of the so-called vaccine and in so doing they broke every traditional ethical guideline that exists.

I repeat, none of this had ever happened before. And yet it all happened at the same time, all around the world and it all followed a predictable pattern.

(I predicted most of it months, if not years ahead, just as I accurately predicted that the death total in 2022 would be staggeringly high. The lockdowns caused many deaths but the covid-19 jab has been, and will continue to be, a significant cause of death. The number of heart problems, including myocarditis, and strokes is now a real worry. And the jab has resulted in immune system damage which makes individuals more susceptible to infection. The incidence of infectious disease deaths is going to continue to rise. The climate change cultists, who steadfastly reject all genuine science, will doubtless try to blame this on global warming!)

You might have thought that even the trusting and slightly dim witted would have raised at least one eyebrow at what was happening. No sane person could possibly believe that all these extraordinary things were merely bad luck or coincidences.

The truth is that it is all about control. A group of people whom I call conspirators (because that is what they are) and who consist of bureaucrats at the United Nations, bureaucrats working for the European Union and a variety of Non-Governmental Organisations (NGOs), the secretive Bilderbergers, leading bankers and a group of manipulative, greedy billionaires, want total power over our lives. They want to take away our freedom. They want to reduce the size of the global population (which they believe is too large) and they want to introduce a social credit system with which they can control everything we do. They want to bring in a single, global currency and force us to live digital lives – with everything we do controlled by computers, robots and apps. And since having even a little money gives us independence and freedom, they are determined to take away our money.

They know that in order to take total control over our lives they must use fear to create chaos and uncertainty. They know that routine makes us feel secure and comfortable but chaos and uncertainty make us anxious, depressed and fearful. The cabal of conspirators has deliberately made us insecure. To succeed, they must destroy everything that we are accustomed to, and our way of life must be smashed. They know that they must break us as humans and take away our humanity and our natural sense of compassion. And they know that they must destroy the world economy as it exists. And then they will lead us into the Great Reset, the New World Order, the new normal.

The really sad thing is that most people won't ever believe that really terrible things are happening on purpose because they cannot conceive that anyone would do the things that the bad people are doing. (This was a human weakness exploited by Adolf Hitler and the Nazis who deliberately took advantage of people's innocence and refusal to accept just how evil some people could be.)

What is not understood (or has been forgotten) is that governments, NGOs and charities cannot help those who are in need either well or efficiently. Charles Dickens showed this very vividly in the 19th century and nothing has changed. Institutions and their bureaucratic employees have always been designed to crush originality but, worse still, they are also designed to crush kindness. History has shown that the only permanent cure for pain and distress is kindness, and that is being crushed out of our society by the collaborators; people who do what they are told to do and whose only role in life seems to be to be compliant. The collaborators are largely ignorant but always invariably cowardly because they never ask the questions any sensible person would ask. Their ignorance is, perhaps, forgivable. Their cowardice is most certainly not.

Here is one very small example of how kindness is being crushed and legislated out of existence. Local councils have designed their car parks in such a way that users who leave a car park earlier than they expected when they purchased their parking ticket cannot pass their ticket, with its unexpired time, onto another motorist. Indeed, this is now illegal and forcing motorists to put their number plate details onto their ticket means that motorists who do show a moment of generosity (which doesn't cost the council a penny) are likely to find themselves in court.

Everywhere we look it is clear that either the lunatics have taken charge or else we are victims of a massive on-going conspiracy.

For over a decade central banks have been 'printing' money (or, rather, merely pretending to print it) on an unprecedented scale. Interest rates have been pushed lower than ever before in history. For several years huge amounts of money were invested at negative interest rates. Governments around the world have more debt than ever and are struggling to pay off the interest payments on their debts. There is little or no hope that they will ever be able to pay off the debts themselves. Taxes are at an all-time high. As a result of all this, investment professionals and individual investors have taken to gambling and putting their savings (or, in the case of the professionals, other people's savings) into reckless projects which can hardly be dignified by the name 'investment'. Billions have been funnelled into crypto-currencies such as Bitcoin and traditional controls have been absent.

There have been many financial crashes and crises over the last century and a half. The years usually remembered as having notable crashes were 1873, 1896, 1907, 1929, 1972, 2000 and 2008. Every time there has been a crash it has been a result of a lethal mixture of greed and stupidity, speculation and irresponsible actions by investment companies and banks, all exacerbated by a lack of control by governments and central banks.

Never before, however, have things been as bad as they are today.

In the last decade, the world's central banks have proved themselves to be either corrupt, incompetent and irresponsible, or determined to destroy currencies, investments, banking and the world economy. Politicians have endorsed and promoted their actions.

It is essential, by the way, to remember too that our politicians aren't just crooked (I doubt if any profession has more members in prisons than politicians – not even lawyers are as bent) but they are also frequently staggeringly stupid. It wasn't that long ago that David Lammy, who is, as I write, the UK Labour Party's offering as Foreign Secretary, once claimed on a television programme called Mastermind that the English King Henry VII somehow managed to succeed Henry VIII. Lammy was a convinced supporter of the value of the covid-19 jabs (he announced that they were safe and they worked) though I do wonder how much of the research he had studied in depth before publicly announcing his support for the new product. He was just one of a long list of celebrities who enthusiastically endorsed the jabs – though I rather fear that most of the celebrities had probably spent as much time looking into the facts of the vaccine as I have spent learning about flower arranging. Just how Mr Lammy claims to know that the vaccine is safe and works is beyond me but everyone who followed his advice should know that when he appeared on the television quiz show I've just mentioned, he was asked to give the married name of scientists Marie and Pierre who won the Nobel Prize for physics in 1903 for their work on radium. Lammy's reply was Antoinette. (He presumably got Marie Curie mixed up with Marie Antoinette.) When he was asked for the name of the building used as a prison by Cardinal Richelieu he named Versailles instead of the Bastille. This is a man who served as a government minister. And Lammy once criticised the BBC for wondering whether the smoke from the Vatican would be black or white when the cardinals were selecting a new Pope. He seemed to think there was an element of racism in this well-known way of announcing if a new Pope had been elected. The thing about Lammy is that he didn't seem aware of the extent of his ignorance. Maybe he had been conducting secret private clinical trials in his purpose built laboratory. Maybe he's got a time machine which enables him to see into the future? Or, perhaps, he said the covid-19 vaccine was safe and it worked because someone in the Government said it was safe and it worked. Lammy was and is supposed to be a member of Her Majesty's Opposition. His job was and is to question the Government and to protect his constituents. But he rolled over and let the vax supporters have their way with him.

I suspect that many people (particularly those under the age of 40) still have no idea just how bad things can get.

In the 1970s, the collapse of the stock markets was worse than the Wall Street Crash. The UK stock market fell 70% between April 1972 and November 1974. In the US, stocks fell by 50% between January 1973 and October 1974. These collapses followed President Nixon ending the link between the dollar and gold in 1971. Prior to 1971, gold had a fixed price of $35 an ounce but America didn't have enough gold to cover all the money it had printed so fiat money (without any gold backing) was invented and became worldwide. This was also the end of the fixed exchange rate. The values of gold and oil duly rose by 15 fold. It was, of course, the rise in the price of oil which caused most commotion.

The words 'this time it's different' are traditionally defined as the most costly four words in history but this time it really is different. We are heading into the deepest, darkest economic depression in history and it is quite clear that the problems have been deliberately created. As things stand at the moment all the savings and investments in the world are at risk.

The billionaires and the Bilderbergers and the members of the World Economic Forum will, of course, simply continue to get richer and richer.

Everything in this book will show how, little by little, the conspirators (and their assistants – the collaborators) are doing everything they can to ruin the global economy and to lead us into the digital prisons of the Great Reset.

You may notice, by the way, that some details are repeated at different places in the book. This is done deliberately, where figures relate in different ways to different issues, to draw attention to important points and to help put the many different issues in perspective. The alternative was to have lots of cross references (see page 000 and so on) throughout the book. This always seems to me to be inconvenient to the reader. It's vital to remember that the conspirators have been planning this fraud for decades and they have created an incredibly complex web of deceits; deceits which affect every imaginable aspect of life.

Vernon Coleman, January 2023

1.

I am painfully aware that the majority of people (probably around 80%) still believe what they have been told by their governments, by the drug companies and by the medical establishment. There are many science deniers who still believe that there was (or is) a pandemic, that the covid-19 'vaccine' saved millions of lives and that without widespread vaccination programmes infant mortality rates would rival those of a century ago.

The science proves these claims to be wrong, of course, and if free and open debate were allowed it would not be difficult to expose the lies that have been told for what they are. But free debate is banned today and media organisations such as the BBC have in the past openly boasted that they refuse to allow any discussion of vaccination in general or of covid-19 jabs in particular. (The BBC's particular and peculiar boast was that they would not allow anyone to question vaccination on a BBC programme 'whether right or wrong'. Just how the BBC's directors fit that policy in with their charter and their commitment to be fair, open and honest is something they must one day be asked to explain.)

Similarly, the bankers and the politicians and the mainstream journalists insist that the recession into which we are now blundering was a result of misfortune following covid-19 and Russia's invasion of Ukraine.

Those who prefer to believe that the regulators, the central bankers, the politicians, the trade unions, the health professionals and the mainstream journalists around the world are all making the same egregious errors, at exactly the same time, are, of course, free to stick with their beliefs. I would not dream of censoring their views – however absurd they might be.

But In the end, whether you believe that we have been overtaken by a barrage of coincidences or that there is a conspiracy behind everything that is happening, there is no difference in what has happened, what the results are and what you must do in order to survive.

2.

At the end of 2022, it was reported that in the UK and other European countries such as Sweden and Denmark, just 1% of financial transactions involved cash. The same was true in Singapore.

In the UK, half the population reported that they had had difficulty paying for goods or services with cash. Councils are replacing car park cash machines with apps which can only be used with a smart phone. (If your local council introduces car parks where you can park only by using an app, make sure that you complain. I believe those councils are probably breaking the law and you should appeal if you get fined.)

More and more cafés, restaurants and shops are refusing to accept cash. It's difficult to travel using cash. *Which* magazine recently said that we need to avoid sleepwalking into a society in which cash users are excluded. They're wrong. We're not sleepwalking into anything. We're being deliberately, mercilessly driven into a cashless society, and those people who pay for coffees and newspapers and snacks with a credit card are the worst kind of collaborators. Even worse is using an app on your phone to pay for a coffee.

In December 2022, I looked hard for a little cheery news about cash and I found this. In Italy the new leader, Giorgia Meloni said that currency notes are the only legal currency in Italy and that electronic money doesn't count. Her first budget will include a rule that allows shops and businesses to refuse plastic and demand cash for payments up to 60 euros. I hope she's got good protection.

We are very, very close to losing cash and if we do it will be the beginning of full-blooded social credit and a digital society. Without cash they will know everything and they will control everything you do.

The half-witted say 'Oh, what a pity it is that cash is disappearing', with no conception of why cash is disappearing. The fact is that cash is the key to everything. The conspirators want an entirely digital society. When there is no cash they can cut off your access to your money in an instant. Note that I said 'cut off your access to your money'. Look what happened to the Canadian truckers whose bank accounts were frozen because they dared to protest. Video sharing platform Bitchute had its accounts closed by its bank.

There can be no possible doubt that one of the main and most urgent aims of the conspirators is to get rid of cash and to force us to deal only with digital money. The aim is to create an entirely digital world where everything we do is digital and where without smart phones and computers fitted with a variety of officially approved apps, we can do nothing.

There is much blindness about just what we are going to lose when cash disappears. Some folk are merely concerned with the superficial, sentimental loss.

A columnist in the weekly magazine *Country Life* wrote this:

As a boy, I was occasionally given a penny to spend and with it I bought four Fruit Salads, a sweet, chewy bundle of joy…there was a lot of pleasure to be had from a quarter of a penny in the 1960s. In the 1970s…we were given a token for five pence to spend in the town's sweet shop. You could blow four pence on a Mars bar, but I bought an assortment of Refreshers, Opal Fruits and Fruit Salads'. By the 1980s, cash machines had become commonplace, yet it took me a while to stop marvelling that you could stick a card into a wall and money would come out. Cash was king…Now that I do everything on my phone, I find it slightly surreal. Cash will apparently be gone for good in a decade, I will miss it.'

This blind failure to see just how terrifying our world will be without cash appals me.

And yet there are plans everywhere to get rid of cash as quickly as possible. This was not difficult to predict. I've been warning about the demise of cash for nearly two decades. In my first video, which was released in March 2020, I stated that the coronavirus hoax and the much promoted fake pandemic, were being introduced for three reasons: to help get rid of older people; as an excuse to bring in compulsory vaccination programmes; and to get rid of cash.

When cash is no longer available we will all be forced to use digital currencies; and to pay for everything with plastic cards or with chips inserted under our skin. (This has already been tested in several countries.) A cash free society is a dream shared by dictators and totalitarians.

The European Commission wants to set lower and lower limits on cash payments. For some years now banks in the UK, and within the EU, have asked customers to explain what they need the cash for if they try to take out more than an arbitrarily allowed sum. (I always say that I want the cash to buy sweets. The bank clerk always writes this down on their form.) It has for some time been against the law to pay large cash sums into a bank and anyone who tries to do so will, at best, find themselves facing a barrage of intrusive questions.

Supporters of this robust and indefensible clampdown on freedom argue that there is a link between the amount of cash around and the incidence of criminality but this is completely false. In practice there is no correlation between the availability of cash and the incidence of crime or tax evasion. Indeed, most criminals now operate online, and forcing everyone to do more and more of their transactions through the internet will mean that more and more people will become victims of online scams – which will, in many cases, result in huge losses. My daily junk mail regularly includes a couple of dozen scamming attempts from crooks telling me that 'my parcel is ready for collection if I send my bank details'; 'that I am due a TV licence refund if I send my bank details'; 'that a Nigerian Prince will send me £100 million if I send my bank details'; 'that I am due a tax refund which will be sent to me if I send my bank details'; 'that my favourite supermarket wants me to collect the fridge I have won but will I please send my bank details' and 'that my bank believes my account has been compromised and I should send my bank details so that a check can be made'.

In Denmark, the Government wants to get rid of cash completely on the laughable grounds that it is expensive for banks to handle. This policy is also coming in throughout the Scandinavian countries with Finland, Sweden and Norway all following suit. The argument against cash also includes the totalitarian point of view that cash enables citizens to move around without the state, and myriad large companies, knowing exactly where they are at any time of day or night, what they are doing and what they are buying. (All of this information is, of course, vital to a police state and valuable to companies who can use the information to help them sell products and services.)

Removing cash and introducing digital currencies (controlled by an app on your smart phone) will give the State total control of your money. The Bank of England has already boasted that it can use a crypto-currency to force citizens to buy only certain products (and to prevent them buying products of which it does not approve). They actually promoted their new crypto-currency as useful for parents who wanted to control what their children bought with their pocket money. This is the essence of the social credit scheme. If the State decides that you are too fat, it will stop you buying chocolate or cake. If the State decides that you are drinking too much alcohol, it will bar you from buying wine, beer or spirits. And, it is also clear, that a crypto-currency, controlled by the State and the banking system, can be turned off if you do not satisfy social credit requirements. Also, of course, it has been made clear that citizens will not be allowed to save any of their digital money. Just as phone companies 'steal' the money in your mobile phone if you don't make enough calls, so banks will 'steal' the money you have earned if you do not spend it. If you think that sounds far-fetched you should know that there are already some banks which fine people if they keep their money in their bank account. Governments (and banks) don't want their citizens to save their money. They want them to spend it to keep the economy growing – so that they can increase their tax take.

I repeat: when digital currencies replace traditional currencies there will be an expiry date on the money you earn. If you don't spend the money soon enough it will disappear. It will be impossible for workers to save any money at all. You won't be able to leave digital money in your will.

Those who are sceptical, and who still trust the authorities to do 'the right thing', might like to remember that my warnings about smart meters have proved accurate. When smart meters were introduced I warned that the power companies would use them to turn off supplies to customers. This is exactly what has happened. Customers who miss a payment, and who have had a smart meter fitted, are likely to find that their energy supply is halted and that to obtain further supplies they must pay in advance.

And, of course, physical bank branches are closing rapidly. Every time a bank closes another branch (usually done with the self-serving excuse that their customers all want to bank online) we move closer to a cashless, digital world.

3.

We rely on our politicians (and the regulatory agencies they provide – with our money and on our behalf) to control the financial institutions and to ensure that there is some degree of stability in the world of finance.

However, the regulators (and the politicians) have betrayed us so consistently that it is now impossible to believe that the betrayals have not been deliberate.

Whenever there are clear signs of malfeasance among bankers and investment professionals there will be a tightening of the rules. The regulators who failed to prevent entirely predictable financial horrors will beat their chests, promise to do better next time, and tighten the rules which have never worked in the past. Lobbyists working for the big banks and investment companies will make sure that there are no serious restrictions.

In the autumn of 2022, a variety of new measures were proposed in the UK which were, allegedly, designed to control the investment and banking industries. The proposed measures were worse than useless and included a new policy allowing building societies to obtain their funding from the wholesale markets – instead of relying on deposits left with them by private savers. This, of course, was exactly the same process which led to the disastrous collapse of Northern Rock in 2007 and the change will put small investors (and, ultimately, taxpayers) in great peril.

Another proposed change, removing the protection of ring fencing (whereby investors' savings are kept separate from the money investment bankers are using to gamble with) will allow banks to be more risky and more daring – using investors' money to help increase their gambling stake. The profits from this gambling will accrue to the bank and to the individual bankers (in the form of bonuses). If the gamblers lose money the bank shareholders will suffer but the gamblers themselves will lose nothing. The gamblers can only benefit from their gambling. It's moral hazard; risk free profit; akin to going to a horse race and making a bet in the knowledge that if your horse wins then you will keep the winnings but that if your horse loses then someone else will pay for your loss. All this will ensure that the poor and slightly well-off will lose whatever money they have while the obscenely rich will become forever richer.

Sir John Vickers, who headed up the post-crash commission on the banking sector, has warned that relaxing ring fencing rules in this way could be 'an extremely dangerous and wrong path for us to follow'. You bet it will be. The only beneficiaries will be millionaire bankers. The only losers will be small investors and pensioners.

It is worth noting that even with the regulations the UK has at the moment, there have been clear signs that bankers have learned nothing from the last few decades. Santander was recently fined £108 million for money laundering and NatWest was fined £264 million for breaking the rules.

4.

I have been concerned about the disappearance of cash for some years.

Here, for example, is what I wrote in 2006 for my book *How to protect and preserve your freedom, identity and privacy.*

'There was a time when shopkeepers welcomed cash payments. No more. In most countries it is now illegal to pay more than small bills with hard currency. Try to pay with cash and you may well find that your offer is refused. Even if your cash is accepted the chances are growing that your suspicious behaviour will be reported to the authorities. Cash is no longer king.

Why?

Simple.

People who pay by cash are able to move around relatively anonymously. They don't leave a paper trail of receipts behind them.

The authorities don't like that. They like to know where we all are. Plastic money puts us all in the power of the bureaucrats. They can find us whenever they want to find us. They can see where we've been, where we are and where we are going. They can see what we've spent and what we've spent it on.

All this information is invaluable to tax collectors, of course. And it's also invaluable to companies who want to sell us things and services – and to make money from us.

Cheques will be the next to go. Some banks in Europe have already stopped issuing their customers with cheque books. Once again, the explanation is that cheques make life easier for terrorists.

This is nonsense, of course. The fact is that banks can't make much money out of cheques. They have to issue cheque books free of charge. They much prefer credit cards which enable them to charge huge fees – and to keep a computerised eye on their customers' spending habits.

The claim that by stopping us using cash and cheques they are somehow helping to protect us from terrorism is nonsense. Terrorists will still use cash (though they may not shop at the sort of places that are likely to 'shop' them to the authorities). And terrorists will use credit cards without ever having to worry about being traced. They use credit cards in false names and they use stolen credit cards.

And when they want to change cash they (like the money launderers) will use currency change booths (available all over the world) and they will then transport the proceeds by purchasing high value items such as rare postage stamps.

If the authorities don't know this then they are unbelievably incompetent. If they do know, then they know that all the bizarre and intrusive demands they make (two gas bills, a shot gun licence, your passport and so on to withdraw your own money from the bank) are a complete waste of time, designed to bewilder and confuse the vulnerable rather than to stop the malignant terrorist.

Taken from *How to protect and preserve your freedom, identity and privacy* by Vernon Coleman 2006

5.

And here is what I wrote for my book *Living in a Fascist Country* in the same year:

'Everyone must report cash transactions to the police. If you buy a car with cash, pay for a holiday with cash, buy furniture with cash then you will be considered a possible money launderer and reported to the authorities. They must report you or they will face prison. Banks cooperate with the authorities. If they think any of your transactions are suspicious (and that's a very subjective thing) they will tell the Government. If you sell your car for more than £3,000 and pay in the proceeds as cash you will be reported to the authorities as a possible criminal.

America has introduced regulations (which are, of course, now slavishly followed by the British authorities and by British banks) which are said to be designed to catch money launderers, criminals and terrorists. (They aren't, of course, but that's what they say they are for.)

If a bank thinks you might be guilty of something they must send either a Suspicious Transaction Report or a Suspicious Activity Report to the authorities. They will not tell you that they have submitted one of these reports. Even if the teller is your best friend they will not tell you. They are not allowed to.

What counts as suspicious?

a) A refusal to provide identification. A bank can ask you for as much identification as it wants. If you decline to give information you will instantly be branded as either a terrorist or a money launderer.

b). Refusing to offer an explanation. If a snotty, spotty bank employee asks you why you want money or where money has come from you are obliged to tell them. Otherwise they will probably file a Suspicious Activity Report or a Suspicious Transaction Report.

c) Running a bank account with a third party – particularly one who is absent. So, for example, if you run a bank account for an aged relative who can't get to the bank then there is a good chance that the bank will regard you both as potential terrorists or financial criminals.

d) If you put more money into your bank account than you would normally earn then your bank may well snitch on you. So, if you win money at the dog track or sell an old painting for a tidy sum, and are then silly enough to put the money into your account, you will attract attention.

e) Not knowing or being ignorant of charges, rates or taxes will brand you as a financial criminal. (Yes, I know it's stupid. I know that no one – not even bank employees – can keep up with all the charges. And I know that financial criminals are likely to be completely au fait with all the rules.)

f) If you buy lots of gold coins you will automatically be reported. As I write the limit is £5,000 worth in a single transaction or £10,000 during the space of a year.

g) If you have money but no apparent income you will arouse suspicions. So, if you are living on income which goes into another bank account or you are living on your savings then you will be regarded as a terrorist, criminal or money launderer.

h) Something called 'structuring transactions' gets bank employees and Government snoops very excited. You are structuring a transaction if you divide it into smaller pieces. The authorities will assume that you are doing this to avoid attention. So if you and your wife or husband goes into the bank together and both order some foreign currency for your holidays then you will trigger a secret investigation. If you and your wife or husband or a friend go into the bank together and then go to separate tellers to conduct your business separately, the transactions may be suspect.

i) If you ask a bank clerk about the bank's policy on record keeping, disclosures or reporting then you will be suspected of wanting to do something illegal.

j) Don't talk about politics to a banker, broker, financial advisor or accountant. Don't complain about taxes. Don't discuss financial privacy either. All these things could lead to a secret investigation.'

Taken from *Living in a Fascist Country* by Vernon Coleman published 2006.

6.

Governments around the world have massive, unprecedented, debts but they are still throwing money around as though they are desperate to bankrupt their countries – which, of course, they are.

To make things worse, in both the US and the UK, over half the population now rely entirely on money from their government. (They are, effectively, receiving the universal basic income which is part of the plan for the Great Reset.)

In the United States, President Biden is planning to cancel student loans that are outstanding – expecting taxpayers' to cover the massive losses. In Europe, the bureaucrats are subsidising energy costs with billions of pounds of taxpayers' money. Germany, for example, spent over 50 billion euros protecting one energy company from collapse. In the UK, the Government has spent huge amounts subsidising and protecting energy companies.

Also in the UK, the Government is doing everything it can to protect the 28% of households who have a mortgage, at the expense of the 72% who don't.

In Australia, household debts have risen to terrifying heights with the debts totalling 202% of net disposable income. Lots of borrowers there face rapidly rising mortgage costs (with their payments going from 2.5% to 6%). Many will be unable to meet the new cost and will go bankrupt.

In Canada, which was at the start of 2023 arguably the riskiest and most dangerous economy in the world, economists were forecasting a 30% decline in house prices.

The destruction of the economy and the move towards the mantra 'you will own nothing' is travelling apace and it is occurring globally.

7.

Most of today's financial commentators in the media seem to have little understanding of inflation (possibly because they are too young to have experienced the effects, perhaps because they are too ignorant to know what has happened in the past and probably because they are merely parroting the nonsense fed to them by the conspirators) and most seem convinced that within a few months or so of the start of 2023 (when this book was written) the current high inflation levels will drift back down to what they regard as 'normal'. They also assume, quite wrongly, that interest rates will go back to where they have been for the last decade. They are quite wrong about that too.

Just about everything the Government has done has produced yet more inflation. Deciding to raise benefits in line with inflation (running at over 10%) ensured that public sector workers (traditionally the greediest workers in the UK) would demand considerably more than inflation. Handing out huge sums of money to help private home owners and businesses pay for their fuel ensured that the Government would have to put up taxes massively. Creating a fake war with Russia (which has never been declared but which is costing taxpayers tens of billions of pounds a year in bombs, bullets and tanks which are being provided free of charge to

Ukraine) pushed up inflation. Providing furlough payments during the crazy lockdown period also created a massive amount of inflation. If governments really wanted to cut inflation they would cut their spending, stop borrowing money, stop printing more money and put up interest rates to a sensible level. Their current policies seem designed to weaken currencies and drive up inflation.

Even as inflation soared in Europe, the European Central Bank continued to print money (they call it quantitative easing) through their bizarrely named Pandemic Asset Purchase Scheme – buying 100 billion euro bonds every month to try to bail out the insolvent bits of the European Union. Interest rates were still being kept low and were indeed negative for much of the time. (Negative interest rates mean that banks charge depositors to look after their money.)

Printing money (as central banks have been doing for a long time now) goes hand in hand with inflation and is guaranteed to lead to disaster. High inflation in Germany led to the Nazis taking power. High inflation in Russia led to the Bolsheviks. And high inflation in China led to Mao, the little red book and the communist revolution. High inflation has, in recent years, destroyed Argentina, Venezuela and Zimbabwe – to name just three. The millennials and Z generation won't know this but in the 1970s, in the UK, inflation averaged 13% for most of the decade and hit a peak of 27% in 1975 when the pound collapsed under all the excitement. I remember being thrilled to obtain a business loan (so that I could buy the building I used for my publishing house) at a mere 16% interest.

The consequences of today's inflation will be devastating. The next generation (and the generation after that, and so on and so on) will pay the price. And since future generations will not have voted for their debts, today's governments are creating a new version of taxation without representation.

High inflation always destroys the lives of those who have savings but the very rich (the billionaires) will become ever richer as their assets grow in value at the expense of everyone else.

The one final certainty is that prices of goods and services will never go back to what they were – even if inflation stops rising.

8.

'Invest in inflation. It's the only thing going up.'
Will Rogers

9.

Governments lie about inflation.

First, they claim that inflation is a rise in prices which is outside their control, and which they are struggling to hold back. This is the first lie. Inflation is caused by governments printing more money, and devaluing the stuff that is already in existence. If the Government doubles the amount of currency in circulation then it halves the value of the money that's already out there. And that pushes up prices. So governments cause inflation.

The second lie is the size of the problem. Inflation is usually much higher than they say it is. This is because the official figures usually exclude luxuries such as housing, energy and food. Education, pensions and healthcare are also routinely omitted – even though these are, for many people, the biggest costs in their budget. It is for this reason that people whose income is inflation-linked (people with inflation-linked pensions or private pensions depending on index linked gilts) find life difficult. In order to retain your spending power (and your quality of life) you need to make much more than official inflation levels from your investments – otherwise your capital is shrinking. So if you don't take risks you are going to become poorer.

When the official level of inflation is 10% the real level of inflation will be at least double that. This means that if you are earning less than 20% a year on your investments, you are losing money. All this means that unless you are very rich, or are prepared to accept a deteriorating standard of living, you have to take some chances with your capital. Government policy means that you really don't have much choice. Moreover, it is vital to understand that inflation figures are now crooked and that the inflation figures governments talk about bear no relationship to the real inflation figures.

Inflation has a powerful effect on investments. Rising inflation is toxic for shares and for bonds. When inflation goes up interest rates also rise and governments tighten up monetary policy. When inflation falls, share prices and bond prices tend to go up, and sometimes soar. The huge bull markets of the 1980's and 1990's were a consequence of the fact that inflation was falling from the high levels of the 1970's. Many investors who did well during the 1980's and 1990's still believe that their success was 'normal' and to be expected. Some actually believe that they are entitled to gain 15% returns from their portfolios for ever more.

Here are some things you should know about inflation:

1. Inflation was kept down at the end of the 20th Century because western countries were importing cheap stuff from China. Cheap television sets, cheap bras and cheap shoes. This helped enormously in the 1980's and 1990's. It meant that we could buy more stuff with the money we had in our pockets and our bank accounts. But the Chinese workers now want higher wages. They want motor cars and they want television sets of their own. So the inflation rate in the West was bound to rise.

2. The rate of inflation has a vital influence on the economy. Rising inflation means that interest rates have to go up (or must, at the very least, be kept at their current level). Rising inflation also means that monetary policy must be tightened. Falling inflation, on the other hand, results in lower interest rates and a booming economy. If inflation is not considered a threat central bankers can, if they think it is necessary, reduce interest rates in order to stimulate a stagnant economy. But if inflation is considered a threat, central bankers will usually keep interest rates fairly high because they will be worried that if they lower interest rates too much they will over-stimulate the economy and produce more inflation. (Governments constantly claim to have found the way to conquer the 'boom and bust' economy. They are lying, of course.) The bull market of the late 1980's and 1990's followed the high inflation rates and big bear of the 1970's. It was the falling inflation rates that drove the powerful bull markets. As inflation fell and productivity went up (as a result of new technology and as China and India started manufacturing things) so we did better and better. Cheapish oil made everything very easy. Those were the days when investors got, and learned to expect as normal, returns of 15% a year on their equity investments. If you wanted your money to grow there was no other game in town. Just buy shares and sit back and wait. And you didn't have to wait long.

3. In the middle of the 20th Century, governments undermined the value of our money (and discouraged savings) by printing too many banknotes. The more money in circulation, the less the money is worth. (Because there is a finite number of things that can be bought with the money in existence). Today, the amount of money in circulation (in the form of real notes) is only a tiny amount of the money available. Banks are now creating money by lending it as a debt (with interest attached, of course) and it is that practice which has really pushed up inflation. The whole problem started when bankers and politicians got rid of gold as a basis for our currencies. When governments could only print as much currency as they had gold, the politicians were restrained. When the link with gold was abolished, governments were free to print as much money as they wanted. Then they made things even worse by using computers to create seemingly endless supplies of 'imaginary' money. It's hardly surprising that house prices have been rising (with occasional slumps) for decades. The last birthday card I bought cost more than my first car. That's inflation. Inflation really does eat away at savings.

4. Paradoxically, politicians and central bankers love some inflation. The reason is simple. When the value of money goes down a little bit, debts get washed away. If you are a government with huge debts then inflation is a wonderful thing. It helps diminish the value of your debts as time goes by. (By the same principle, inflation helps reduce the value of debt for everyone else, too.)

5. Rising commodity prices usually result in a rise in inflation in countries which have to import commodities. Countries which produce the commodities which are rising in value usually do well. I have been long-term bullish about the price of oil and other commodities for decades (commodities of all sorts are running out and the demand for them is rising inexorably). I therefore believe that high inflation is likely to be a consistent problem in countries such as Britain (which rely on importing commodities such as oil).

6. Inflation hit nearly 15% in the USA in 1980. (It was much higher in the UK.) This was a direct result of America's 1971 decision to abandon the link between the dollar and gold. Freed from the need to back up their dollars with gold, the American Government printed more and more dollars. And the dollar became increasingly worthless. Will inflation ever get back to those now

seemingly absurd levels? Why not? Governments are still printing vast quantities of currency and backing up their banknotes with nothing but hot air. It seems inevitable that the value of currencies just about everywhere should continue to shrink. And that, after all, is all that inflation is.

7. Inflation means that for most people their salaries and wages have failed to rise for many years. People think they are better off than they were twenty years ago. But when inflation soars it enables workers to have pay rises without the pay rises actually costing anything. People aren't really better off because costs have risen faster than pay.

8. Governments don't just ignore rising costs in essential purchases when they are assessing inflation figures. (They fiddle the figures in this grotesquely dishonest way because it is easier to keep the official inflation figures down – and to convince everyone that they are doing a good job – if they don't count the things that are going up most.) They also use astonishing little tricks such as including hedonic adjustments and rental-equivalent home pricing and using geometric averaging when working out different varieties of inflation.

Geometric averaging means that if the basket of goodies measured to find the inflation figure contains one item which goes up 10% and another which goes down 10% the effect on the basket isn't 0% (as you might imagine) but a 1% fall. Governments produce this miracle of accounting by multiplying 110 (the figure obtained because of the 10% rise) by 90 (the figure obtained because of the 10% fall). This gives a total of 99. And, lo, a fall in inflation (and the cost of living) of 1%. Only politicians and economists can do this. Hedonic adjustments enable politicians to take advantage of progress to keep inflation low. If you bought a computer a year ago for £1,000 and you replace it with a computer which costs £1,500 but is 10 times as fast then the computer is registered by the Government as costing less even though it really cost more. And rental-equivalent home pricing? That's a trick they use to minimise the effect of rising house prices (when they include them). If your home is now worth twice as much as it was a few years ago but the rent you would have to pay has only gone up by half then the inflation figure is deemed to be a half. The real rise in the cost of the home is ignored. All these utterly, deplorably, dishonest inventions were designed to enable politicians to lie and cheat the voters. There are more tricks: for example, when they measure gross domestic product they tend to ignore the fact that the population has grown and that the per capita GDP – the figure that really matters – is probably going in the other direction. Unravelling the lies they tell can be tiresome work. The lies have worked very well on both sides of the Atlantic. Politicians and civil servants are concerned only with what they can get away with. They ignore the moral and ethical dimensions. Businessmen and women who lie usually fail eventually (though they may get exceedingly rich before they fail). Investing in companies run by crooks can damage an investment portfolio. But politicians who lie (and lie well) usually do well. The electors consistently choose the politicians who lie most convincingly.

9. Inflation is an invisible tax. Although it is a boon for borrowers (the £250,000 borrowed to buy a house shrinks as a result of inflation) it is a curse for savers (the £250,000 pension fund shrinks in value and purchasing power as a result of inflation). Pensioners and others on a fixed income lose out because their buying power is constantly being eroded. Earners whose income doesn't match inflation (the real figure, rather than the false 'official' figure) also lose out. They may seem to be getting richer, as their income grows, but in reality they will be getting poorer. And everyone who pays tax will lose out. Tax thresholds do not usually rise with inflation. So stamp duty on house purchases affects an increasing number of people as house prices rise and the stamp duty thresholds remain the same. And since the point at which taxpayers find themselves liable for higher rates of tax tends to stay the same (or to rise nowhere near as much as inflation) the number of people paying higher tax rates is rising rapidly. You will probably not be surprised to learn that governments don't usually take inflation into account when helping itself to a share of your income. So, if you have a 6% income on your investments and tax rates are 40% you will pay 40% of your 6% to the Government. That leaves you with a 3.6% return. But if the official level of inflation is running at 5% then you are losing 1.4% a year. If real inflation is 10% you are losing 6.4% a year. You may think you are getting richer but in reality you are getting poorer.

10. In August 2008, Zimbabwe issued a Z$100 billion note to keep up with inflation (then running at 2.2 million %). That was not, however, the highest denomination banknote produced in the last

100 years. In the 1920's, Germany had a 100 trillion Papiermark note. And in 1946 Hungary, printed notes with a face value of 1,000,000,000,000,000,000 pengos (that's one followed by 18 zeros and it is known to its friends, if it has any, as a quintillion). One German I know recently pointed out to me that his father had taken out an insurance policy in 1903. Every month he made payments. The policy was for a 20 year term and when it matured he cashed it and took out the proceeds. He used the entire proceeds to buy a single loaf of bread. A Berlin publisher reported that an American visitor tipped their cook one dollar. The family met and it was decided that a trust fund should be set up in a Berlin bank with the cook as beneficiary. They asked the bank to administer and invest the dollar. The price rises in inflation-crazy Germany became dizzy. A student at Freiberg University ordered a cup of coffee in a cafe. The price on the menu was 5,000 marks. He had two cups. When the bill came the price for the second cup of coffee had risen to 9,000 marks. He was told that if he had wanted to save money he should have ordered both cups of coffee at the same time. The printing presses at the Reichsbank could not keep up. Factory workers were paid daily at 11.00 a.m. A siren would sound and everybody gathered in the factory forecourt where a five ton lorry waited. The lorry was full of paper money. The chief cashier and his assistants would climb up onto the lorry, call out names and throw down bundles of notes. People rushed to the shops as soon as they had caught their bundle. Doctors and dentists stopped accepting currency and instead demanded butter and eggs. When the Germans introduced a note for one thousand billion marks hardly anyone bothered to collect their change. It wasn't worth picking up. By November 1923, a single dollar was worth a trillion marks. People living on their pensions found that their monthly cheque would not buy a cup of coffee. People dependent on insurance payments were destitute. When traced back, it is clear that hyperinflation in Germany started when Germany abandoned the gold backing of its currency in 1914. The Government borrowed to finance the war. Half a century later the Americans borrowed to finance the Vietnam War (their philosophy was identical: the war will be over quickly). And since America left the gold standard and started borrowing big time, inflation has been a constant and serious problem. (Though the extent of it has been ignored and suppressed.)

11. It is partly because of their unspoken fear of inflation that ordinary people throughout the world have unwisely (but understandably) relied on buying property as a defence and a way of preserving wealth. In spring 2007, the Japanese Government sold a two year bond which promised to pay interest of 1% a year. This was the highest bond the Japanese Government had issued in ten years. When governments flood their countries with money that doesn't cost much to borrow (because interest rates are kept low) they are deliberately creating inflation. When money is 'cheap' people buy more houses. Between 1985 and 1991, houses in Japan rose by 51% before the bubble burst. Similar things have happened in America and the UK. In America, where interest rates were kept low, house prices rose 90% between 2000 and 2006. And then the bubble burst. In the United Kingdom, where interest rates were also kept low, house prices rose 118% between 2001 and 2007. Many so-called experts dismissed thoughts that this was a bubble and claimed that house prices could, and would, continue to rise indefinitely.

This section was adapted from *Moneypower* by Vernon Coleman, published 2009

10.

'Last year if you didn't eat, didn't drive to work, didn't heat your home, didn't visit a doctor, didn't buy a house, didn't buy insurance of any kind, didn't have a child in college and didn't pay ...taxes, your cost of living agrees with the Government's cost of living index.'
Clyde Harrison

11.

Printing lots of new bonds (and ultimately lots of new currency notes) is an easy way to improve your exports. It was started in earnest by the Americans in the 1990's. It works because when you print more currency you lower the value of the stuff already in existence. And when the value of your currency falls when compared with the currencies of other countries your exports become cheaper. All the world's major powers have for years been increasing their money supply. It is hardly surprising that some currencies such as the British pound have been on a downward slide for years. The American dollar has lost more than seven eighths of its purchasing power over the last 60 years.

12.
'Inflation is like sin: every government denounces it and every government practises it.'
Sir Frederick Leith-Ross

13.
Negative real interest rates occur when inflation rates are higher than interest rates. If a saver receives 2% in interest but the inflation rate is 10% then the saver is losing 8% of his money every year. This is not a normal phenomenon since savers usually demand that interest rates rise above inflation for this very reason. But for years now, since the crash of 2008, this has been exactly what has been happening – with interest rates at or below 0% and inflation notably higher. Since 2022 things have become notably worse with inflation reaching double figures and interest rates hardly budging above zero. Anyone who has saved will have seen their savings fall in purchasing value. This problem has led many savers and investors to put their money into high risk investments – often with the chance that they will lose not just part of their money but all of it. Millions have seen their rainy day savings and their pension funds decimated by this deliberate, cold-blooded process.

14.
Ridiculously low interest rates, meaning that savers end up losing money, have meant that many have been attracted to high risk 'investments' with crypto-currencies such as Bitcoin among the most fashionable. Dozens of new crypto-currencies have been promoted (often by celebrities) and there have been regular stories of people losing money. One unfortunate buyer lost his Bitcoin collection

when the hard drive containing millions of pounds of coins somehow ended up on the local rubbish dump.

Studies have shown that the most enthusiastic purchasers of crypto currencies such as Bitcoin are young males – with those between the ages of 18 and 29 being the most enthusiastic. Sadly, the majority will have lost money on what they will have thought of as their 'investments' but which were, in truth, no more than gambling stakes. Some of those who bought crypto currencies will have undoubtedly lost all their money. There has been much fraud and much stealing.

During 2022, the overall value of the crypto currency market fell from $3 trillion to $800 billion. This capacity for fraud means that it is hardly surprising that central banks have talked much and often about introducing their own crypto-currencies.

Many people (me included) regard crypto-currencies as nothing more than a pretty joyless way to gamble (without the drama and colour of the race track or the casino) but crypto-currencies such as Bitcoin seem positively stable and sensible when compared with Non Fungible Tokens (NFTs) which have also become a fashionable investment fancy in recent years.

The mania for buying NFTs seems to me to bear an uncanny resemblance to the mania for buying tulip bulbs which was fashionable in the Netherlands in the 17th century when traders bought and sold tulips for astronomical sums.

When you purchase a NFT you pay out good money to purchase a piece of artwork that only exists on a computer. You can buy an NFT for almost anything. For example, you could buy an NFT confirming that you were the first person to buy a copy of this book or the first to listen to the latest song by an artist you've never heard of. You can't touch what you've bought, you can't print it out or do anything with it other than tell people that you have it.

15.

Towards the end of 2022, *The Economist* magazine suggested that property prices in the UK could fall by more than a third. They'll fall everywhere in the world.

And the Bank of England has been gaming a scenario in which house prices fall by 33% and the unemployment rate rises from 3.5% to 12%. The Bank seems to think that the banks will be able to cope with that sort of economic collapse.

Lloyds Bank, rather more optimistically, said in 2022 that it was preparing for house prices to fall by 20% in 2023. Goldman Sachs warned that billions of pounds could be wiped off the value of commercial property in the UK alone as a direct result of the Government's activities.

Naturally, a collapse in house prices will hurt home owners, damage consumer confidence and damage banks.

A one third drop in house prices means that a £300,000 house will be worth £200,000. Most home owners with mortgages will be 'under water' – they'll owe more on their home than it's worth. Remember the World Economic Forum: you will own nothing and be happy.

And mortgage rates are going to stay high. They're never going back down to where they were.

16.

The conspirators who want to take over the world (the unelected bureaucrats at the United Nations, the unelected, self-appointed 'leaders' at the World Economic Forum, the unelected bureaucrats at the European Union and a collection of unrepresentative and deeply unpleasant billionaires) have for some time been planning to herd those world citizens who are left into large cities where they will live in what will effectively be large prisons. Planners around the world have already made moves in this direction.

For example, in Singapore the State has almost complete control over what housing is built, where it is built and how it is built. The Singaporean Housing and Delivery Board builds flats which are leased to citizens. The leases allow the citizens to remain in their flats for their lifetimes but upon their death, the Board takes back the flats and resells them. Already, 78.3% of Singaporeans live in these HDB flats. There are very tight restrictions on foreign ownership, and homeowners must pay an annual property tax calculated according to their property's hypothetical rental income.

In France, new 15 minute cities are being created so that 'all the essential services a person needs are within a 15 minute walk'. Paris is already working on this scheme which is, effectively, a way of creating new ghettoes. The socialist mayor Anne Hidalgo has introduced schemes which are disliked or loathed by many locals and which are driving foreigners out of the city. (My wife and I sold our much-loved apartment in Paris in part because of new regulations which were clearly designed to force out foreign owners. So, for example, foreigners living in the city had to pay special taxes. The new rules also meant that the bureaucracy was expanding and the city was being destroyed. Many small shops and cafes were shutting down and the city was becoming an increasingly unpleasant place in which to live.)

A similar 15 minute scheme is being introduced in Oxford, England.

Politicians are introducing these schemes without the approval of residents – and even despite their opposition.

In Japan, an enormous conglomerate called Hankyu Hanshin is, with government approval, building a new district in Osaka which will contain shopping malls, offices, hotels and residential apartments. The aim is that residents will be able to live, work and shop without leaving their district.

The Dutch Government has committed itself to the climate change fraud, demanding that every primary resource in the economy be recycled in some way. This means that builders must use recycled materials, and there is a building materials passport to help developers. The Dutch Ministry of Economic Affairs and Climate Policy requires organisations to take energy efficiency measures with a payback period of five years or less. What this means in practice is that if a more energy efficient product appears on the market, the developer must switch to that new product if it would earn them back their money within half a decade.

In October 2021, the UK Government published the targets for its 25 year environment plan. Much of this plan seemed to be dedicated to 'mitigating and adapting to climate change' – a cultural myth, built on rhetoric, hysteria and pseudoscience, which the Government seems to have chosen to accept as scientific fact.

17.

In the UK, where home ownership is more traditional than any other country, house prices have been deliberately forced upwards by a variety of insane government policies. The result is that whereas the average house price in England and Wales was four times annual income in the year 2000 (and that was considered rather high) it has risen to well over nine times annual income. It is hardly surprising that young couples find house purchase nigh on impossible. Higher interest rates and mortgage rates will bankrupt millions of home owners but it seems unlikely that even a notable fall in house prices will tempt young people into home ownership.

The WEF's infamous threat: 'you will own nothing and you will be happy' is coming true.

Well, at least the first half of it is coming true.

18.

Governments are using every trick they know to impoverish their citizens and to raise taxes as fast and as high as they dare.

In the UK, the Government is using fiscal drag to further impoverish millions – in other words they are leaving tax bands unchanged so that an increasing number of people move into higher tax rates. Today, even some teachers, nurses and policemen will be paying higher rate tax, and before long several million workers in the UK will be paying income tax at 62% (a little known tax rate which is triggered when incomes hit an arbitrarily fixed level).

The UK Government is also keeping the Value Added Tax (VAT) threshold at £85,000 for small companies. (This is now similar to levels throughout Europe.) The result will be 100,000 more small businesses will be dragged into the VAT net.

When VAT was first introduced, only the higher earning small companies and sole traders were obliged to join up. Today, almost all small companies will be obliged to register for VAT. An annual income of £85,000 sounds substantial but if a small company employs two or three individuals, even minimum wage can push gross earnings levels up to this sum. (The £85,000 is gross and includes all the company's expenses.)

Forcing small, growing companies to register for VAT is destructive in a number of ways. Those running these companies are forced to do their accounts digitally every three months (meaning a good deal more paperwork and, probably, expensive accountants fees). Companies are also forced to buy special accounting software.

The big problem is that VAT registered traders must add the 20% VAT rate to their charges and this means that small companies no longer have any advantage over large companies. Many small companies which are forced into the VAT scheme go bankrupt because the extra administration means that they can no longer compete with big companies which have their own departments to deal with all the forms which must be completed every three months.

There will be two results.

First, a good number of people running small businesses will work less, in order to keep their income under the £85,000 figure. This will mean that it will become increasingly difficult for home owners to find local tradesmen.

Second, a huge number of small businesses (the sort which might eventually become big businesses) will go bankrupt. There is some irony in the fact that Britain is now outside the European Union but that this has always been a deliberate policy within the European Union. The EU was, of course, designed in part to further the interests of large companies and to suppress and eventually destroy small businesses of all kinds.

19.

The 2008 financial crash was either a result of total and quite unprecedented incompetence by central banks, regulators, leading investment houses and politicians or it was a result of a deliberate plan to destroy the global economy, impoverish untold millions and force millions more into poverty and homelessness.

Bankers everywhere invested in incredibly risky assets which few of them understood and regulators allowed the housing market to spiral completely out of control. Individuals who had no jobs, no income and no savings were given mortgages and allowed (or, rather, encouraged) to 'purchase' several expensive properties. Increasingly complex financial instruments were invented and sold by hucksters who had no idea what they were selling to investors who had no idea what they were buying.

Governments around the world bailed out the bankers (most of whose banks were heading for bankruptcies) with huge lorry loads of taxpayers' money. The bankers grabbed the 'free' money but instead of using it to compensate investors, or to correct some of the damage they had done, they used it to give themselves massive bonuses and enrich themselves still further. Only one banker was punished. Most were rewarded for their dishonesty.

If anyone has to be held responsible for this obscene display of greed it must surely be the financial regulators who allowed all this to happen – none of whom was ever disciplined or punished in any way.

After 2008, regulations were introduced to try to control the banks and, theoretically, to prevent such terrible things happening again. The regulations had very little effect, of course, though a cap was introduced on bankers' bonuses. The cap was so ineffective that in many cases it actually resulted in bankers earning even more money than before. The cap was removed in Truss and Kwarteng's curious budget in the autumn of 2022 and was the only change that was left untouched by Sunak and Hunt. Sunak formerly worked at Goldman Sachs. Kwarteng worked at J.P.Morgan Chase and at a hedge fund.

And now, despite or because of the new crisis which has been created (again, either as a result of gross, universal incompetence or through deliberate policies designed to impoverish and destroy) the UK Government is considering relaxing rules which were introduced to separate investment banking, and other high risk operations, from high street banking. The rules were introduced to protect small investors and savers and the aim was to force banks to put capital aside so that they could absorb potential losses without destroying the lives of ordinary, small investors or requiring huge amounts of money from taxpayers.

By removing these rules, the Government will free the banks to spend the money they put aside (or, in politician's parlance 'to release some of that trapped capital'.)

It is worth noting that big European banks (including the four biggest UK banks) are actually considered so risky and so dangerously poised that their share prices value them well below their asset value. So, for example, the share price of Barclays bank discounts the assets of the bank by around 50%. The share prices for Lloyds Bank, HSBC and NatWest are similarly well below their book value.

20.

Environmental, Social and Governance (ESG) regulations are another weapon being used by the conspirators to destroy the global economy. Financial journalists are as caught up in the Big Con just as much as health journalists are and today, instead of looking to see if a company is profitable and efficiently run and being fair to workers, customers and shareholders, woke journalists worry about whether or not a company takes a responsible attitude towards climate change. It is, of course, these same financial journalists who, despite evidence which proves the contrary, believe that drug companies are honourable and that the vaccines they have produced have saved the world.

Investors are now being told that they must take notice of a company's devotion to ESG requirements when considering a possible investment. This is utterly absurd. And even more absurd is the fact that 'acceptable' investments include drug companies (the most immoral companies on earth) companies such as Alphabet (which owns Google and YouTube, undoubtedly two of the world's most evil companies) and companies such as Tesla (which has been much criticised) whereas supermarkets (which provide a vital service) and miners (without which there would be no electric vehicles) and oil companies (without which there would not be anything much) are regarded as unsuitable investments.

Unfortunately, companies are being pressured into taking absurd actions because multiple small pressure groups are buying a few shares and then trying to force companies to behave as they would like them to behave (with absolutely no deference to the democratic process), often adopting destructive policies which, in the end harm workers, pensioners, customers and shareholders.

Devotion to ESG has destroyed many big companies as bosses, who are often frightened of being targeted by extreme cultists, court left wing woke popularity and try to wrangle themselves a knighthood or better.

In truth, companies have but three responsibilities: to the workers (and pensioners); to the customers who buy their product or service; and to the shareholders who have invested money in the company and made the whole thing possible. As long as they obey the law and all regulations relating to their responsibilities towards workers and the environment, companies do not have, and should not be expected to have, further responsibilities to the wider community.

Recent surveys have shown that employees and investors aren't in the slightest bit interested in artificial ESG requirements. Workers want their company to treat them fairly, and shareholders want the company to make a profit (so that their investment can earn them a fair reward). As a result, ESG is becoming increasingly unpopular with workers, shareholders and even customers (whose priorities tend not to include ESG policies) and yet governments are introducing yet more laws and regulations forcing these unwelcome, useless and often damaging policies on companies.

Nevertheless, some countries are giving up on ESG more or less completely. And several very large investment companies have walked out of the NetZero group and announced their disaffection for ESG in all its forms. In the US, where investment companies seem better run, a number have criticised ESG allegiance. The attorney general of Missouri announced in October 2022 that the Missouri State Employees' Retirement System had pulled $500 million in assets from BlackRock because of the investment group's social and political agenda. The attorney general pointed out that the group's fiduciary duty should outweigh considerations linked to stakeholder principles. Another 19 state attorneys general expressed similar concerns, and the governor of Florida confirmed that the State's treasury division had started to pull $2 billion in funds from BlackRock.

Britain, however, appears to be increasingly committed to this damaging, pseudoscientific nonsense – a nonsense which will help destroy companies, severely damage pension funds and cause needless widespread impoverishment.

In Britain, investment and pension companies seem to consider that their allegiance to the nonsense of ESG is of greater importance than their fiduciary responsibility to the investors whom they represent and whose money they are paid look after. Investment professionals act as though their responsibility is to the happiness of ignorant climate change cultists rather than to the investors and pensioners whose futures they control.

So, for example, I was particularly dismayed to read that Legal and General and HSBC (a bank which I wouldn't consider as either a customer or an investor) have apparently signed a resolution, to be voted on at the next annual meeting of mining giant Glencore, to ask how the company's development of thermal coal mines meets the goals of the 2015 Paris climate agreement. I don't understand why those two companies don't just invest elsewhere. Glencore is a big mining company. It digs stuff out of the ground – including coal. If you don't like that then shouldn't you just invest somewhere else? Personally, I'm happy for miners to take coal out of the ground since it helps keep us all alive. (And, for the record, the British Government recently approved a new coal mine in England. Oh, and burning wood pellets, which is now an approved activity, causes significantly more damage to the environment than burning coal.)

Even more alarming is the fact that governments and courts are now interfering and ordering public companies to forget about their responsibilities to employees, customers and shareholders and to do more to appease the senseless, pseudo-scientific fears of climate change hypocrites.

Some may think this is all happening through ignorance or by accident.

But those who can see what is happening know better.

21.

Brexit (Britain leaving the European Union) has been blamed for all Britain's ills though in reality, of course, it is responsible for none of them. The way politicians dealt with the fake pandemic and the designer war into which our political leaders have drawn us are responsible for the very real economic problems now facing us.

Brexit is massively unpopular with those who support the European Union – whose numbers include most of the country's leading civil servants, business leaders and politicians. The EU's supporters are desperate for Britain to reverse the Brexit process and to rejoin the EU, with or without the support and approval of the electorate.

Because those opposing Brexit have most (if not all) of the power, little or nothing has been done to take advantage of the country having left the EU.

And the potential advantages still remain.

The country could (in addition to saving untold billions of pounds – the fees paid into the EU to support the bureaucracy and to pay charitable donations to southern European countries), arrange new trade relationships with other countries and it could get rid of the thousands of irrelevant, restrictive and damaging regulations which the European Union has been churning out for decades.

I detailed the disadvantages of the EU, and the advantages of leaving in my book entitled *OFPIS: The truth about the EU*.

In my book entitled *The Shocking History of the EU*, I explained how the EU was founded by former Nazis with the deliberate intention of continuing Hitler's work after the end of the Second World War.

Brexit has failed (so far) because the conspirators wanted it to fail. Indeed, they needed it to fail – to punish the British electorate and to warn off other disenchanted voters elsewhere in Europe. It is important to remember that the European Union is, and always was, an essential step towards the Great Reset.

Remainers (the intellectual dwarves who would like Britain to go back into the most fascist union ever created) like to forget that the British people would have never voted for the Lisbon Treaty if they'd been given the opportunity. They ignore the fact that the euro was designed purely to force through political integration and create a sample for the world government the EU's founding fathers (a bunch of despicable Nazis) yearned to foist upon the people. The EU is littered with examples of fraud and corruption and this has been the case since the very start.

If the next British Government is an alliance between Labour, Liberals and the Greens, their enthusiasm for the European Union, the Great Reset and Net Zero will probably mean that Britain will apply to re-join the EU – quite possibly without another referendum. Net zero, by the way, is the most chilling piece of legislative nonsense ever created – worse than China's insane net zero covid policy which is, of course, deliberately designed to improve compliance with the tyrannical social credit system.

The result of such an alliance will be ever increasing social and economic chaos.

22.

When Andrew Bailey was made governor of the Bank of England in 2019, he already had a rather scandal rich history from his time as head of the Financial Conduct Authority.

His time at the Bank of England has been even more disastrous.

In 2022, inflation seemed to surprise the Bank, even though it was so predictable that in 2020, 2021 and 2022, I regularly predicted that the problem would be upon us and would become a real problem. I find it alarming to realise that Mr Bailey and his huge overpaid staff couldn't see the inflation coming – and do something about it. (The obvious 'something' being to raise interest rates.)

Under Bailey's supervision, the Bank of England failed to support the Government of Liz Truss, with the result that gilts crashed and pension funds lost a great deal of money. Some pension funds lost half their value and I suspect that many workers who are expecting to be able to retire with a decent pension do not yet know how much money their fund has lost. Large companies lost tens of billions of pounds from their pension funds – and that money is being replaced at the expense of shareholders.

The Bank of England bought gilts at their most expensive, acquired much of the Government's debt and has been selling the gilts cheaply. It now makes losses every time it sells gilts. (This error will, it is estimated, cost taxpayers £133 billion.)

It should be said, however, that this problem is not unique to the UK. The Bank of England owns 40% of UK gilts and in the US, the Federal Reserve owns 25% of US Treasuries.

Bailey was so inept that it didn't seem to him inappropriate to tell workers not to expect much of a pay rise when he himself was being paid over half a million pounds a year – with an absurdly generous pension to look forward to.

23.

'Since we decided a few weeks ago to adopt the leaf as legal tender, we have, of course, all become immensely rich…But we have also,' continued the management consultant, 'run into a small inflation problem on account of the high level of leaf availability…so in order to obviate this problem,' he continued, 'and effectively revalue the leaf, we are about to embark on a massive defoliation campaign, and…er, burn down all the forests. I think you'll agree that's a sensible move under the circumstances.' The crowd seemed a little uncertain about this for a second or two until someone pointed out how much this would increase the value of the leaves in their pockets whereupon they let out whoops of delight and gave the management consultant a standing ovation.'
From 'The Restaurant at the End of the Universe' by Douglas Adams

24.

For many years now, there has been a steady two way traffic between Goldman Sachs, the discredited American bank, and governments and official bodies all around the world. At the time of writing, for example, Sunak, the British Prime Minister is just one of many Goldman Sachs alumni prominent in public life.

I don't think the words 'honest', 'moral', 'public spirited' or 'decent' would be recognised by many as appropriately describing the staff of Goldman Sachs.

25.

Their plan is to make every one of us bankrupt and they're well on the way to succeeding. Only the billionaire conspirators are likely to avoid this. The conspirators must be delighted at the way things are going.

The rising cost of food and energy will eat into our savings. Those without savings won't be able to put anything aside. Every penny will go into paying for basic essentials. Company earnings will be devastated by poor production figures (exacerbated by strikes, working from home and the bizarre new fashion, popular with the young, for doing as little work as possible) and so investments and pensions will go into a long, slow dive. The coming recession will quickly turn into a depression.

And, remember, nothing is happening by accident.

Interest rates will continue to rise, and millions who have mortgages will find that they can no longer afford to pay for their homes. The result will be a fall in house values. And as values fall so those mortgage problems will get worse. It won't be long before millions have a bigger mortgage debt than their house is worth. Their homes will be re-possessed and they will be left with huge debts. Alternatively, the Government may say: 'We'll take over your mortgage and you can stay in your house…but you will no longer own it'. Remember, none of this is happening by accident. It has all been orchestrated.

And those with savings won't survive either. Although interest rates will rise they won't go high enough to defeat inflation. If interest rates go to 5% and inflation is 15% then investors and savers will lose 10% of their wealth every year.

Within a remarkably short space of time the conspirators will have succeeded in destroying the wealth and independence of tens of millions of people in the UK and hundreds of millions around the world.

There will be no middle classes. The elderly will die in penury. The young will never own a home or have the security of having some savings. The conspirators want us bankrupt because they know that money gives us freedom and independence.

In practical terms, the only way for many to protect themselves is to downsize, to reduce their debts and their outgoings and to be prepared for a simpler way of life.

Sadly, too many of those who understand the crisis we are facing, and the horrors of the Great Reset, the disappearance of cash, the advance of a digital world and the social credit paradigm, simply shake their heads, settle in front of the television and do nothing to stop it.

26.

Gordon Brown, one of the UK's discredited former Prime Ministers, is back. He has produced a new report full of advice for Labour leader Sir Keir Starmer.

Brown's suggestions include:

Scotland should be allowed to borrow more money

A council should be established to bring together regional political leaders. (Regional leaders were an EU suggestion years ago – rejected by the voters.)

Empowering digital industries

Getting rid of the House of Lords. And then replacing it with another second chamber called the 'Assembly of the Nations and Regions'.

Brown is one of the scariest of Britain's former politicians. I cannot think of anything Brown did which made Britain greater. But I can think of a lot of things he did which buggered up British life. (Flogging all Britain's gold at a rock bottom price was particularly moronic.)

Here is a section from my book *Gordon is a Moron* in which I explained how Brown's obsession with 'targets' helped remove humanity from public life and in particular to destroy the health service.

'How Brown's Performance Target Culture Has Destroyed Public Services

1

Brown is a believer in performance targets. It is, therefore, his fault that public services have been afflicted by an absurd and dangerous 'target culture'.

Brown seems to believe that if you give public servants targets they will work harder and provide a better service. Indeed, like any good soviet dictator, Brown seems to believe that he only had to announce a target for it to become an achievement.

Brown has set spending review targets (known as public service agreements or PSAs) which cover the performance of all the major government departments and which set highly complex and specific criteria for the way in which public servants are assessed. The PSAs cover everything from exam results to crime figures and cancer rates.

What Brown didn't realise (possibly because of a lack of much genuine work experience – he's been an MP since the age of 32) is that when you give public servants targets they will concentrate on satisfying those targets to the exclusion of everything else. Self-preservation takes over, the target becomes the aim and the focus, and the welfare and indeed the existence of the public, the individual, the person, the end user, the patient, the client, the poor taxpayer hoping to get some service for their money, goes out of the window, never to be seen again. The end result is a massive fraud. Public servants are encouraged to cheat the public in order to get promoted and to receive bonus payments.

Performance indicators on a scale that would have impressed Stalin have been forced on councils, schools, hospitals, the police and institutions throughout the nation, and Gordon the Moron has helped create a mad bad world in which every public employee is more concerned with meeting 'targets' than in satisfying the public's needs.

It was Gordon Brown who created the entirely mad world in which public services can claim that they are providing the public with wonderful service even though everyone with half a brain knows that they are not. It was Gordon's target culture which encouraged administrators in every branch of public service to cheat and to concentrate not on providing a good service but on satisfying Gordon's utterly absurd targets.

2

Gordon Brown's endless series of targets gave him control over other Government Departments and the way they worked. By controlling the purse strings at the Treasury, and making other departments obey his targets, Gordon interfered with other departments in a way never seen before in Britain. Brownism meant that a bunch of people who knew nothing about vital services such as health, education and crime fighting were effectively in control of health, education and crime fighting. Incompetent professionals were able to behave ever more incompetently. Unimaginative, uncaring jobs-worth bureaucrats who worked by the rule book were able to rise through the ranks and take control. For them Brown's targets were a dream come true. Politically correct nurses, policemen and teachers now all had excuses for ignoring the needs of their patients, citizens and pupils. Millions of public servants who were being paid to serve the public now had just one master: Gordon. Instead of pleasing the public all they had to do was meet their artificial targets and success and glory would be theirs. It is to their eternal shame that so many professionals should submit so meekly to such nonsense.

3

Some of the targets introduced were nothing short of mad. So, for example, the Atomic Energy Authority was told that it must increase its favourable media coverage by 43.9%. Kew Gardens was told that it must receive 30,000 herbarium specimens a year.

4

Hospitals were told that patients who visited casualty departments had to be seen within four hours. (I confess that I always found this woefully unambitious. Can you imagine Gordon Brown sitting in a casualty department waiting four hours to have a member of his family seen by a nurse? No, nor can I.)

Hospitals got round these woefully unambitious casualty waiting time targets by employing a 'hello' nurse. The nurse just says 'hello' but doesn't offer any treatment. But she is officially the end of the waiting time.

Struggle into a Brownian casualty department with a leg hanging off and a nurse will totter over and say 'hello'. That's it. Hello. You can sit there and bleed to death. No one cares. You've been seen within four hours. It is deceitful and dishonest and so it fits the Government's style like a rubber glove.

In other hospitals the result of Brownian targets is that patients wait for seven hours because they are placed in 'medical assessment units' where, although they still haven't been treated, they don't officially count as still waiting.

5

Before April 2004, GPs provided out of hours patient care, including weekends and bank holidays. But then the Labour Government offered GPs a new contract which entitled them to opt out of providing 24 hour a day 365 days a year cover for their patients. (It was this new contract, which also enabled GPs to dramatically increase their incomes well into six figures. The Government, under Gordon Brown's financial guidance, negotiated a deal which, by 2007, gave GPs an average income of £118,000 – an increase of 63% on what they were earning when they had to work nights and weekends.) The overall result of the change was that the cost of providing out of hours care doubled and the quality of care provided for patients slumped dramatically.

6

The NHS as financed by Gordon Brown spends £1.5 billion a year on management consultants but cannot afford £2.50 a day for drugs needed by patients with Alzheimer's disease. The drugs which English patients are denied can delay the progress of symptoms such as memory loss and personality changes. (Patients living in Gordon Brown's home country of Scotland get all the drugs they need. Gordon Brown would receive drugs for Alzheimer's Disease if he needed them because he is Scottish.)

The organisation which banned the drugs is called NICE (the National Institute for Health and Clinical Excellence). NICE was set up by the Labour Government in 1999 to decide which medication and treatments should not be made available to patients in England and Wales.

7

The elderly are now treated as irrelevant and disposable in the British NHS. I frequently receive mail from readers telling me that they have noticed that as they (or their relatives) reach certain age milestones (seventy is the one most commonly quoted) medical care is withdrawn. Patients who are considered 'too old' are quite likely to be denied investigations and treatment. It doesn't matter how fit they are – they will be left to die simply because of their biological age. Age discrimination has been officially authorised by the Government which has effectively institutionalised ageism.

In the modern NHS the most vulnerable patients are the ones who are being abandoned and being denied the most basic care. I have a file of reports detailing instances in which patients have been treated with unbelievable callousness by nurses and administrators. And, indeed, I have witnessed this sort of reprehensible behaviour at first hand. It sounds absurd but I have stood in a British teaching hospital and watched in horror as nurses ignored pleas from patients who needed bedpans or were unable to feed themselves and were forced to lie, hungry, and stare at food which had been cruelly and tantalisingly placed in front of them but which they could not eat without help – help which never came. The number of patients leaving NHS hospitals suffering from malnourishment rose by two thirds in the last half of Gordon Brown's Chancellorship. In 2006, an astonishing 2,265 people left hospital lacking basic nourishment. In 2001, the figure was 1,381. In some areas of Britain nearly half of hospital patients report that they don't get enough help with eating.

And, while patients lay starving, a total of 13 million hospital meals were thrown away untouched. Between 2001 and 2006, hospital food costing £162 million was thrown away – not just because it was inedible (which much of it was) but because patients were too ill to eat it without help and no one was prepared to help feed them.

8

A recent survey from Help the Aged shows that 144,000 old people never leave their homes. This is sometimes because they are too frightened to go out. It is often because they can't afford to go out. Over a fifth of pensioners now live in poverty.

9

GPs are now paid according to whether or not they 'hit' their targets. So, for example, GPs search over assiduously for hidden ailments and now frequently label patients as having disorders they do not have, and coerce them into taking drugs they do not need, in order to hit their own targets and to earn more money. Today's GPs no longer have a direct responsibility to their patients but, too often, regard their patients as a means to an end – the end being the number of patients they can diagnose as being diabetic, treat with blood pressure lowering drugs or treat with cholesterol lowering drugs. Brown's accursed targets have destroyed what was left of the traditional doctor-patient relationship.

10

Cleaners at an NHS hospital were told to turn over dirty sheets instead of using fresh ones between patients. The Good Hope Hospital in Sutton Coldfield, which recorded 36 cases of MRSA and 327 cases of patients infected with clostridium difficile in less than a year, had asked staff to reuse dirty sheets in order to save money.

11

In order to meet financial targets, an NHS hospital in London removed every third light bulb from its corridors to save money. The problem with the NHS is that it has more administrators than nurses or beds. Billions are wasted on poor buying procedures and absurd bureaucracies. The NHS is one of the world's largest employers, with 1.38 million members of staff.

12

Thanks to Gordon Brown, hospitals treat patients with bunions before they treat patients with cancer because bunions are easier and quicker to deal with and so bring down the hospital's overall waiting time. This enables administrators to meet their artificial targets. .

13

Here's another trick hospitals have thought up to help meet Gordon's stupid targets. You need an operation. You're on a waiting list. A nurse or a clerk asks you when you're on holiday. Thinking that this is sensible of them, you tell them when you're away. And that's when they send you the appointment telling you that you can have your operation. Because you're away you don't reply or turn up and the hospital can deal with someone else. But by sending you an appointment they've dealt with you. Two patients are taken off the waiting list. You go to the bottom of the list and start waiting again.

14

Thousands of patients with prostate cancer are being given potentially dangerous drugs quite unnecessarily just to meet targets and clear hospital waiting lists.

The best course of action with prostate cancer patients is sometimes to do nothing – to wait and see what happens before deciding on the best course of treatment. (Often no treatment at all is the best treatment.) But government targets mean that all patients have to be treated within four weeks. And so although some patients are denied the drugs they need, other patients are given drugs they don't need. All thanks to Gordon's performance targets.

How many deaths is Gordon Brown responsible for?

I have no idea.

Nor, I suspect, has he.'

This extract is from *Gordon is a Moron* by Vernon Coleman, published in 2007.

27.

The British Medical Association says that the UK needs nearly 50,000 doctors. This is undoubtedly true now that the BMA has helped ensure that GPs work part time (the average GP works an average of 26 hours a week – and wants that reduced to 21 hours a week) and that hospital doctors work such short hours that there are rarely any doctors in hospitals at weekends.

Any shortage of doctors in the NHS is exacerbated by the number of women doctors who insist on taking a year off work every time they get pregnant. And then, when they return to work, insist on working just two or three days a week. To make things worse, many male doctors who are married to female doctors, take a year off every time their wife or partner gets pregnant.

The decision, made half a century ago, to insist that medical schools recruited more female than male students, makes sense when you realise that the conspirators want to eradicate health care services.

Like scores of other unions, bodies and associations, the British Medical Association, the doctors' trade union, appears to me to be controlled by a cabal of Common Purpose graduates, climate change cultists and far left conspirators aiming to take us into the Great Reset.

(Soldiers have for many years been taught to regard the enemy as sub-human. Prince Harry, in his ghost written autobiography, said he regarded the people he shot as nothing more than chess pieces. The police officers who are used to control demonstrations have been taught to regard members of the public as sub-human. And, sadly, it seems that doctors and nurses have been trained to regard patients as a nuisance and a threat to themselves and the health service for which they work. It is difficult to avoid noticing a pattern here and I find it impossible not to suspect that the heavy hand of the organisation Common Purpose might be responsible in some way or other. Common Purpose has been described as running behaviour modification courses which some people might find rather spooky, to say the least, and, of course, governments now employ professional psychologists with skills in brain washing techniques in order to create fear and other responses which are considered useful. Almost unbelievably, but true, these psychologists have talked openly, and apparently with pride, about the need to create yet more fear among taxpayers – the people who are paying their fees.)

28.

Climate change is a fake concept which was (as I showed in my book 'Endgame') invented to help control the public, to spread fear and to force them to be more compliant.

The fraud has been enormously successful and media organisations have been pressured to accept it as a scientific truth and to refuse to allow any debate on the subject. It has even been suggested that those who question the myth of climate change (who are demonised as 'climate change deniers' to link them to 'holocaust deniers') should be arrested and charged as terrorists. The same bizarre and oppressive suggestion has been made about anyone who questions vaccination.

For those prepared to look beyond the utterly discredited mainstream media, it is clear that the truths about the pandemic fraud, the climate change fraud, the vaccine fraud, the digitalisation fraud and the social credit fraud are all out in the open. It is even clear that many of the computer games popular with children and young adults are designed to prepare the users for a world of social credit. Those who obey the rules win points. Those who disobey lose points.

There are few secrets left and many of those behind the frauds no longer bother to hide their lies and their corruption. Only the collaborators, the doctors who have abandoned the truth as they have abandoned their patients and their honour, and the journalists at discredited organisations such as the BBC who peddle lies and misinformation with the effortless ease of confidence tricksters, are still attempting to pretend that anything that we've been told was anything other than a compendium of lies designed by the conspirators to lead us directly into the Great Reset, the New Normal and a world where compassion, hope, humanity, kindness, decency, and honour have all been replaced by greed, treachery and an endless willingness to sell loyalty and responsibility for the traditional thirty pieces of silver.

The media no longer give time or space to anyone who questions the climate change fraud, even though an increasing number of climate scientists have made it clear that they reject the idea of 'catastrophic climate change' – despite the fact that this will wreck their careers just as effectively as the careers of doctors were destroyed when they questioned the official lies about covid-19. Debate on the issue is banned and the media is constantly filled with lies and fake stories about the threat of climate change.

Towards the end of 2022, government departments in the UK were told to use psychology to change people's behaviour and, as had been done with the fake pandemic and the covid-19 fraud, to use fear to pressurise people into behaving 'properly'.

Governments now plan to put pressure on every aspect of how people run their lives, travel and eat. The tax system is being used to promote the fraud, and people are being forced to change their homes (by installing absurdly expensive new heating systems (such as heat pumps) in place of gas or oil boilers or open fires) and change the sort of car they drive (this is gradually being forced onto people by eventually making them buy electric cars – which have, of course, been proved to be far worse for the environment than vehicles using internal combustion engines).

29.

If global warming ever becomes a reality, instead of a convenient myth used to excuse a growing dictatorship, we should welcome it.

Energy prices are never going back down. Oil is in increasingly short supply and it is going to become ever more expensive to heat homes, offices, shops and public buildings. And maybe they forget to tell you that the EU has absurd policies relating to oil tankers and their insurance which will pretty well guarantee that fuel prices will be higher next winter than they are now. And since fossil fuels provide us with up to 95% of our energy (even when the sun is shining and the wind is blowing) we're stuck with huge energy bills for a long time to come. Those high prices will help keep inflation roaring away at record levels.

During the winters, around 100,000 elderly citizens are going to die of the cold in the UK alone – simply because they cannot afford to keep warm. This, of course, is exactly what the conspirators want. Most of these elderly people are going to die because they cannot afford to keep warm. Throughout the world there will be millions of deaths due to the cost of heating.

Even in the hottest of hot summers, the number of people killed by the heat is only a fraction of that number.

The truth is that we should welcome a little global warming. It would save millions of lives.

Moreover, warmer weather will make it easier for us to grow crops – and to bring down the price of food.

At the moment, global warming is just a convenient myth – a weapon being used in the war currently being waged by the conspirators against the rest of us.

If it ever becomes a reality we should welcome it with open arms.

30.

I reported over 20 years ago that recycling was a scam designed to encourage compliance. Sorting rubbish into different plastic boxes is (much like the fake covid-19 scam) a social credit training programme.

Right from the start, householders have been encouraged to sort all their rubbish and to rinse out all their bottles and cans with fresh tap water – no one encouraging this seems aware that water is one of the world's scarcest and most valuable commodities.

Recycling has, time and time again, been proved to be completely pointless. Much of the plastic that is carefully collected and sorted and then picked up by vast diesel-consuming lorries is exported to China, Turkey, Netherlands and Poland. Much of it is then burnt because it isn't commercially sensible to try to remove the contaminants and turn the material into anything useful and saleable. Just why anyone thinks it is 'greener' to use lorries and ships to transport recycling thousands of miles so that it can be burnt, rather than to burn it at home is a mystery.

Recycling glass is absurdly inefficient because glass is very heavy and uses up a great deal of diesel when it is transported. Yoghurt pots are made of polypropylene and cannot be turned back into food packaging because of food safety regulations.

Collecting food waste in plastic boxes is proving incredibly efficient at attracting rats and enabling them to breed faster and grow bigger. Most communities now have serious problems with huge rats –thanks to recycling.

And confidential papers such as bank statements have been found fluttering around in the street near to dumps.

Recycling was never necessary and always a waste of everyone's time, money and energy.

A friend of mine burns all his rubbish in his garden. He claims that he is being kinder to the environment than anyone who recycles. 'Their rubbish is collected in a diesel lorry, transported thousands of miles and then burnt,' he explains. 'I burn my rubbish here so I do far less damage than the recycling nutters.'

He's right, of course.

Defiance – not compliance.

31.

The conspirators, helped by discredited organisations such as YouTube and the BBC, created global warming as an excuse to stop us travelling. And the plans are progressing well. The Government in the UK was recently advised by climate change cultists in Oxford, England and the inevitable Imperial College that by 2030 all airports in the UK must close except Heathrow, Glasgow and Belfast. And by 2050, the three remaining must go. Until then access to airports must be by rail only.

In Oxford – which now seems to me to be the world centre for insanity born of tyranny – citizens are to be locked into community prisons for most of the year. Before long only the conspirators, politicians and the climate change cultists will be allowed to travel.

No one seems to have noticed that this will create real problems for those citizens who are keen to obey the social credit schemes.

Social credit programmes, as used in China, punish those citizens who do not visit their parents regularly.

Schemes such as the one being introduced in Oxford will make it nigh on impossible for citizens to visit their parents – and to obtain the social credit points they will need if they are to buy food, get jobs and (ironically) to travel.

I suspect that someone in Oxford hasn't thought this through properly.

Governments are now so committed to promoting the absurd net zero philosophy (whereby most people will starve or freeze to death in order to protect planet earth from a non-existent threat) that new laws controlling the way motorists can visit cities are being introduced almost daily. Even when local residents protest vociferously, the new laws are introduced and passed with absolutely no respect for the vestiges of democracy. The green extremists, and their political allies are taking us back to feudal times, the days when few people travelled more than a couple of miles from their home. Special congestion and pollution charges are being introduced everywhere and will hit the poor hardest. The conspirators, the billionaires, the crazed global warming cultists and the leading collaborators will, of course, be exempt from all the laws. The cultists, promoting the pseudoscientific nonsense of global warming, will still travel regularly to their shindigs in pleasant tourism spots. Indeed, the only bit of tourism which will survive will be the special nook which provides aeroplanes and hotels for the hypocritical global warming nutters.

The people introducing these laws know darned well that travel is essential for the economy. If people don't move about freely it isn't just the transport industry and tourism which will be destroyed. Everything – theatres, cinemas, restaurants, health care, shopping centres and even science – depends on people being able to move themselves or their goods from one place to another.

And so everything will change as travel becomes a memory. There will be no point in learning foreign languages. Culture will fade as writers and musicians are isolated. And as the Great Reset becomes a reality, and the global economy dies, so the conspirators will take ever greater control of every aspect of our lives.

32.

There isn't a material on the planet which is loathed quite as much as plastic. But the loathing is nonsensical.

The amazing thing is that politicians insist on ignoring their own experts.

In 2005, the Scottish Government reported that the manufacture of paper bags consumes four times more water than the manufacture of plastic bags. (Water is, of course, one of the most valuable and scarcest commodities on the planet.)

And a 2011 UK Environmental Agency study found that paper bags contribute three times more to global warming than plastic bags. (I don't believe that global warming exists. But cultists who swallow the nonsense should at least look just occasionally at the evidence.)

And yet plastic has been described by as 'one of the greatest environmental scourges of our time'.

Every sanctimonious body in the world seems to believe that their country will be a better place if plastic bags and straws are banned. They prefer to see trees chopped down to make paper bags and little wooden forks.

33.

'A night club in Barcelona called the Baja Beach Club has members who have implanted microchips the size of a grain of rice in their arms. When the members with the implanted microchips arrive at the club, a doorman runs a scanner over his arm, checks his name and photograph and lets him in. Inside the club, waitresses run another scanner over his arm every time he orders a drink.

It isn't new, of course. I've been writing about implanted microchips for years. The technology was first used in the early 1980s when small transmitters were put into the backs of roaming farm animals so that farmers could keep track of them. Just about a decade later, office workers were using radio frequency identification device technology to enter company buildings and to access high security areas. And, of course, many pets have tracking devices implanted under their skin so that they can be identified and returned home if they stray, get lost or are stolen.

In 2001, an American company started developing the idea of chips which could be implanted in humans – both to help track people who had got lost or who weren't where they should be and to provide identification material together with medical records. Fundamental Christians pointed out that this was the 'end of days' since the Bible prophesises that there will come a time when people will have numbers under their flesh. (It's in the Book of Revelations.)

The FDA initially warned that there could be problems with these implantable chips. They might migrate and end up elsewhere in the body; the patient might have an adverse reaction and, in the worst possible scenario, the chip might produce an adverse reaction and be difficult to locate and remove.

And there are two other problems, one big and one massive. The big problem is that hackers could steal your identification number from under your skin and then hack into the computer company's database. Those who promote this scheme say this risk is slight. But maybe they don't know that hackers seem to have successfully penetrated every computer system in the world – including those operated by the American military which does, so I'm told, make something of an effort to stop this happening.

The massive problem is that your government or employer or bank might one day insist that you wear an implantable device so that they can keep an eye on where you are and what you are doing. They will, of course, sell it as an advantage to you – in the same way that speed cameras are called safety cameras.

The implantable chip isn't science fiction: it's real.

The world's first implantable radiofrequency identification microchip for human use (RFID) has now been cleared by the American Food and Drug Administration.

The chip system consists of an implantable micro-transponder, an inserter, a hand-held scanner and a database containing information about the person in whom the chip is inserted.

The chip cannot be seen by the human eye but contains a 16 digit verification number that is picked up when the scanner is passed over the site. The number leads the scanner operator to a database on the Internet. The operator can then get access to whatever information is stored on the internet site. Implantable constantly broadcasting microchips, inserted under the skin, are being used so that the American Government can keep track of its employees and soldiers. The plan is to use them to keep track of visitors to America. You have been warned.'

From *Living in a Fascist Country* by Vernon Coleman, published in 2006

34.

The world is suffering its biggest economic crisis in history. Poverty is global and food and energy prices have reached all-time highs but countries are spending more money than ever on bullets and bombs as the conspirators use war as another tool to suppress and oppress – and indeed to push up prices and increase starvation and energy poverty.

The Stockholm International Peace Research Institute revealed in late 2022 that global military expenditure hit an all-time high of £1.7 trillion in 2021 with the USA alone spending $801 billion

Figures for 2022 will be even higher and military shares in 2022 rose by 20.9% as the rest of the market fell.

35.

The magazine *Accountancy Today* has reported that 515,863 jobs are set to disappear in the UK's finance industry by the year 2030. Automation and technical changes (including robots of one sort or another) will destroy over half a million jobs in banking and finance in the UK alone. The same thing will happen in every other country in the world. Banks, which are expecting to have got rid of cash by then, will be dealing with digital money only. There will be no need for high street banks or for tellers. Big banks and insurance companies will manage with just a few engineers to service their machinery. Bank staff who now regard cash as a nuisance should be aware that without cash they will be unemployed.

But that's the tip of a very large iceberg. Everything I've listed below is going to happen in every country in the world – but it will happen first in the most developed countries. The bottom line is that most jobs are at risk.

Shops, especially supermarkets and large stores are going to get rid of most of their staff within this decade. Automatic tills will replace check out staff and robots will do the shelf stacking. Just look at what is happening already at big warehouses. Deliveries will be made with self-driving vehicles.

Trains and buses will need a fraction of today's staff. The conspirators want to end most travel so there will be no need for trains, buses or other forms of public transport. The idea of a train having a driver and a conductor will be considered laughable, as will the idea of food being served on the train. Any trains which do run will almost certainly be controlled by computer. The unions which are demanding higher salaries for already well-paid staff are merely speeding up this process.

I.T. staff consider themselves irreplaceable. But they aren't. Twitter just fired half its staff (with average incomes of £100,000 apiece). Those ex-employees will be lucky to work again in that industry. All the big tech companies are haemorrhaging staff to cut costs.

Factories will be run with skeleton staffs. There will be virtually no jobs in factories by 2030. Everything will be done by robot.

In the few theatres which will remain, actors and musicians will be replaced by holograms of performers. (This, of course, has already happened.) Film production will use largely computer generated images – thereby saving huge amounts of money – and most jobs in cinema and television will be automated. Entertainment will be provided by computers and avatars. Any software required will be written by computers.

Publishers and literary agents have absolutely no future. Their work can easily be done by computers.

Translating is already done automatically. Books will be routinely translated by computer and audio books will be produced by computer instead of human actors.

Farming will not exist as we know it. The conspirators don't want old-fashioned farms. Using the fake excuse of global warming, they are closing down farms and turning them into nature reserves where wild boar and bison can roam freely. Food will be provided by factories – managed and run by computers and robots. Farmland will become almost worthless. In Holland, the Government has closed 3,000 farms to help ensure that food prices are kept high to save the world from non-existent global warming. The farms that remain cannot afford fertiliser so their food production will fall. If you think any of this is happening by accident then you probably had a brain destroying covid-19 jab. The conspirators must get rid of farms because farms use oil for their tractors and oil is used for making fertiliser. Farmland has no future value whatsoever. If they have their way our diet will be made up of insects and laboratory made food. And I'm not kidding. (Investors such as TV's Jeremy

Clarkson, who bought vast tracts of farmland, hoping that it would hold its value through the generations, might well be in for a very unpleasant surprise if they ever awaken.)

Taxis and delivery services are at the end of the line. Any taxis which are required will be self-driving. Deliveries will all be made by robot carts and drones.

Garages won't exist in most towns. Motor vehicles (whether diesel, petrol or electric) will be banned or taxed out of existence. Only the conspirators and the very high-up collaborators will have access to private vehicles. Most garage mechanics will have no future at all.

House surveys (if required at all) will be done by robots. All deliveries will be done by robot. Hairdressers will be replaced by robots. (If robots can perform surgery better than humans, which they can, they can certainly cut and style hair. They can be programmed to provide the gossip style of your choice).

Tax inspectors will be replaced by computers. Everything will be digital. Taxes will be removed automatically from bank accounts.

Police will be replaced by robots (as they already are in some parts of the world). Snitches and sneaks will take over the role of 'detection' – reporting directly to the courts. Without any traffic there will be no need for traffic police. All that will remain will be a small branch of the military to process the targets of snitches and those citizens breaking social credit regulations.

Health care will have altered completely by the year 2030. There will be no GPs at all. (GPs are already helping to put themselves out of business by working 'remotely'.) Hospitals will be run by robots. As I have already pointed out, it has been shown that robots make better surgeons than people and that robots are more caring and efficient than human nurses. Most doctors and most nurses will be unemployed by the year 2030. Sadly, the health care provided will be an improvement.

(However, robots and computers in medicine will never be able to make off the wall diagnoses – the ones which astound observers with their originality. When I was a medical student, working in Queen Elizabeth Hospital in Birmingham, we had a patient, a young man, who was suffering from prolonged and serious muscle spasms. He was dying. Every consultant in the hospital, and this, remember, was a teaching hospital, had seen him but had been unable to make a diagnosis. Every attempt at treatment had failed. At one point a diagnosis of tetanus had been made but treatment had failed and that diagnosis had been abandoned. Eventually, the one remaining specialist in the hospital was asked for an opinion. He was an orthopaedic surgeon and I don't think anyone held high hopes that he would succeed where everyone else had failed. But the surgeon took one look at the patient and asked why he had an old plaster cast on his left forearm. 'He broke his arm playing football,' replied the registrar. 'The plaster should come off next Friday.' The orthopaedic surgeon shook his head. 'Take it off now,' he ordered. 'Straight away!' The plaster cast was removed and the diagnosis was made. The man's wound had not been properly cleaned. He'd been injured on a grass football pitch and there were still some traces of dirt, with tetanus spores, in the wound. The patient had tetanus with a constant source of infection from the dirty wound. The wound was cleaned and within a very short time the patient recovered. Would a robot or a computer have been able to make that diagnosis? I doubt it.)

Teachers will all be unemployed and all schools and colleges will be closed. All teaching will be done online by computers.

Civil servants will nearly all lose their jobs. Local authorities won't need human staff either. Everything that can be done by a civil servant can be done more cheaply and more efficiently by a computer or a robot. Citizens will be responsible for taking their rubbish to specified collection sites. The rubbish will then be collected by robots.

Mail won't exist anymore outside computers. In the UK, the Royal Mail will have disappeared. All communication will be done online.

All building and most repair work will be done by computer and robot. Architects will be replaced by computers. There may be a little work available for workmen such as roofers and plumbers prepared to access difficult working places – unusual roofs and cellars for example – but eventually difficult to access buildings will be demolished.

Lawyers will all be replaced by computers – as will judges. Everything a lawyer can do a computer can do better. Prisons will be managed by computers.

Newspapers and television won't exist as we know it. What passes for news will be provided by computer controlled websites.

No one will notice. The only radio will be provided by illegal, independent, pirate radio stations run by sole presenters – in hiding and constantly on the run.

So that's the future the conspirators have planned for us.

Those who still think I'm a conspiracy theorist won't have to wait long to find out how wrong they are and how right I am.

If you want to know the truth behind what is happening, read my books *Endgame* and *Social Credit: Nightmare on your Street*. Alternatively, if you'd rather not know what the future holds, go to your nearest sandy beach, dig a suitable hole and put your head in it.

36.

The European Union, founded by the Nazis after World War II is a practical example of the world government which the conspirators are planning. The EU is creating a world suitable for the Great Reset.

And, inevitably, the EU has been corrupt from the very beginning.

Today, the corruption continues. Four prominent EU figures (including the vice president of the EU Parliament, Eva Kaili, were arrested at the end of 2022. There were allegations of bribery by officials from Qatar. Police allegedly seized 600,000 euros in cash and another ten EU parliament employees had their accounts frozen. Kaili was a member of the Progressive Alliance of Socialists and Democrats until she was expelled in 2022.

I suspect EU insiders would regard it as all in a normal day at the European Union.

37.

It has been widely reported that millennials and young people who regard themselves as members of the Z generation are rejecting work. It appears that they have been encouraged by television and social media to believe that they can all become reality television stars, YouTube stars, social media influencers and so on. Many assume that with very little effort they can become exceedingly rich and famous. They don't want to study or work hard. They are disinterested in a traditional career as a doctor, a lawyer or a plumber.

When they realise that it takes a good deal of luck, and a little talent, to become rich and famous overnight they give up and abandon all their hopes. They learn not to care about anything.

Studies have shown that not a few would die if they could do so on television or on the internet. This is not an entirely new phenomenon. A few years ago, a survey showed that most Olympic athletes would take drugs that they knew would kill them within a year if the drugs would help win a medal. Today, a frightening number of youngsters will sacrifice their lives if there is a good chance that their death will go viral.

It is alarming that many admit that they never intend to work. A recent survey showed that 9% of 18-24 year olds say that they have no plans at all to work – ever.

38.

It is a myth that the human race can survive without fossil fuels. After years of heavy investment, the UK still only obtains around5% of its energy supplies from solar and energy sources. And advocates of these two sources of energy always ignore the fact that in pure energy terms these are both of marginal value. Making and running wind farms requires vast amounts of energy (usually sourced from fossil fuels) and when there is no wind there is no energy – and electricity sourced from burning fossil fuels is required to keep the turbines turning so that they don't seize up. Making and running a solar farm is equally expensive in energy terms and, of course, when there is no sunshine there is no electricity. Disposing of wind farms and solar farms when they reach the end of their lifespan requires yet more energy from fossil fuels. (In Germany, wind turbines are being torn up so that miners can get at the coal underneath them.)

The figures for energy provided by non-fossil fuels are skewed by the fact that gas is now officially regarded as a renewable resource and that biofuels (which used to be known as wood from trees) are also regarded as an entirely renewable resource. Those who are enthusiastic about the burning of wood pellets as a source of electricity fail to mention that the cost of cutting and transporting the wood pellets means that bioenergy (as it usually called) is actually a dirtier source of electricity than coal.

39.

Many people now buy what they believe is 'green energy'. They claim the electricity they use has all been created with the aid of windmills and solar panels. Sadly, this is an utter nonsense, and the smug individuals who claim that their laptops and television sets and tumble driers and heating systems are all run with the aid of electricity obtained from renewable sources are deluded.

All the electricity in the UK comes from the National Grid which obtains most of its electricity from fossil fuels. A very small part of it comes from solar panels and wind farms but most electricity comes from burning coal, diesel, gas and wood.

And here's the clever bit: governments everywhere have decided that gas and wood should be redefined as renewable or 'green' sources of energy.

The real irony is that most of the electricity obtained from so-called renewable energy sources comes from burning wood pellets. And the wood pellets come from trees in America. The trees have to be chopped down and turned into wood pellets. The wood pellets then have to be loaded onto diesel powered lorries and taken to a port where they were loaded onto a diesel powered ship and carried across the Atlantic. The whole process uses up far more energy than is produced and is incredibly wasteful. But politicians, journalists and those responsible for selling the wood pellets have succeeded in convincing a very gullible public that this is a 'green' source of energy since trees can, in theory at least, be considered 'renewable'

40.

It is widely believed in the West that coal is yesterday's fuel. This is a colossal myth. In South Africa, coal still provides 85% of the country's electricity, and China has recently been building coal fired electricity generating plants as though there were a competition to see which country could burn more coal which, for all I know, there may well be. And, of course, the UK Government recently approved a new coal mine.

41.

Hydrogen is being promoted by the climate change enthusiasts as the answer to all our problems. They seem to believe that we can use hydrogen as a source of energy and abandon traditional fuels such as oil, gas and coal.

Sadly, as usual, the climate change enthusiasts are ill-informed and over-ambitious. Hydrogen is made by splitting natural gas (which is required for the production process) and produces carbon dioxide which goes into the atmosphere.

So-called green hydrogen is produced by using 'renewable' electricity mostly made by burning wood. And burning wood produces more carbon dioxide than natural gas, pollutes the atmosphere and requires that trees are chopped down in abundance. As the climate change enthusiasts used to point out (before they became enthusiastic about chopping down trees) this lowers the planets ability to absorb carbon dioxide.

The evidence shows that we would all be considerably better off if we went back to burning coal instead of hydrogen.

42.

Miners tell us that we need to make massive investment in new mines and that, indeed, we will need to push up our investment in mining by two thirds higher each year than was being spent for the average for each of the last thirty years. The industry's experts agree that we need between 300 and 400 new mines to find the materials we need.

We need the new mines to find the copper, lithium, graphite, nickel, cobalt and other essential materials which will be required for the heat pumps, electric cars and batteries which are being promised.

But there is a snag.

The climate change nutters have leant on the banks which, as a result, now refuse to lend money for mining exploration or for oil exploration.

And to that problem must be added the fact that politicians around the world are reluctant to allow any new mines to open. Today, it takes 16 years from discovering a possible mine deposit to actually building a mine. Just 20 years or so ago the bureaucracy was bad enough to mean a six year wait. But today the delays are incredible and we will certainly not open the mines which are needed.

The result is that work is going to be delayed or halted.

And, of course, the prices of essential metals is going to soar.

43.

The oil has been running out for years. It was the realisation that the era of oil was coming to an end which triggered the global warming fraud. (If you want to read the full story about the discovery of oil and the way it has changed our world please read my book entitled *A Bigger threat than Climate Change: the End of Oil* which provides all the evidence you'll need to read.)

A bunch of conspirators (including unelected officials at the United Nations, power-hungry politicians and businessmen known as the Bilderbergers and a number of power and money hungry billionaires – later joined by the staff and members of the World Economic Forum) realised that the oil running out would do very serious damage to the world we know.

Oil provided the revolution which took the 20th century out of the Dark Ages.

It was decided that sharing this information with the public would cause many scares and much hysteria. Until my book *Oil Apocalypse* was published a few years after the turn of the century there had been very little public discussion of this problem.

The conspirators decided that in order to cope without oil the global population will need to be cut from many billions down to just half a billion. In order to do this they needed the global population to be culled and the use of the remaining oil to be severely curtailed. And so they chose, quite deliberately, to introduce the entirely fraudulent theory that the world was getting hotter (because of man's activities) and that if nothing was done about it the result would be widespread flooding and general mayhem. When it became abundantly clear that these predictions were unsustainable, the conspirators changed the threat from 'global warming' to 'climate change' – having decided that the broader threat would allow them to blame every entirely normal storm, wind, fire or flood on the new, manufactured threat. (In the UK, builders have been allowed to put new houses on flood plains, and rivers have not been dredged. The inevitable flooding has been blamed on global warming.)

The threat of climate change was built on a remarkable number of blatant lies but, by involving the media in the scam, and by clever use of children as a form of pressure, the conspirators succeeded in promoting their fraud very successfully.

And the lunacy reached extravagant heights when the idea of net zero was promoted and widely accepted by politicians, business leaders and media owners. The idea behind net zero is that some specific time, not very far ahead, we should abandon the use of all fossil fuels and live our lives without them.

There are, of course, serious problems with the whole net zero farce.

Most importantly, there is the fact that if all the world's oil fired power stations and oil fired domestic boilers were closed down tomorrow, the world would still need two thirds of the oil currently being used in order to power trucks, ships, planes and factories. The over-promoted solar farms and wind farms currently provide just 5% our electricity and, sadly, they are pretty useless if the sun is shining and the wind is not blowing. Wind farms, in particular, are of very limited value since it is now generally accepted that they are energy negative – in that making the windmills and building the wind farms use up more energy than they will ever provide. (And that doesn't allow for the energy cost of decommissioning the wind farms when they reach the end of their lives.)

The main source of electricity which does not involve oil, gas or coal, involves the burning of wood. Although burning wood is considerably more damaging to the environment than burning coal, the conspirators and their collaborators have succeeded in persuading politicians and the public that obtaining electricity from the burning of wood is preferable to using fossil fuels.

Oil and gas will not be irrelevant for decades and they will, indeed, have run out long before the currently popular contenders for their replacement are efficient enough to provide suitable replacements.

Despite the problems with cutting down our use of fossil fuels, the conspirators have worked hard in the last few years to make things worse.

Early in 2022, Western governments used NATO to push Russia into invading Ukraine (something Russia had done before, without anyone noticing or pretending to care) and then used the designer war as an excuse to introduce financial sanctions against Russia, knowing full well that Russia would respond by cutting oil and gas supplies to the West – thereby creating shortages and pushing up prices of these essential commodities. Russia also limited the sale of Russian and Ukrainian fertiliser to the West – thereby severely damaging the production of essential food stuffs and putting up the price of food. There is also a huge pipeline carrying oil from Kazakh to the Black Sea which passes through Russia. And the Russians have the power to shut this pipeline. Oh, and the Russians have considerable power over sources of oil in the Middle East – such as Libya.

Western politicians pretended to be surprised and offended by the Russian decision to counter Western sanctions with sanctions of their own. It is difficult to believe that there is a single politician in the West so stupid as to have failed to expect this response.

To make things worse than they already were, the UK's Chancellor of the Exchequer used the UK's budget of November 2022 to introduce an Energy Profits Levy of 25%. Added to other taxes, this levy meant that oil and gas companies would pay 75% tax on all their UK earnings. This was 'sold' to the public as a way of obtaining a windfall tax from the oil companies but it was actually designed to please the climate change cultists by forcing oil and gas companies to reduce investment, to close down exploration projects and to mothball existing oil and gas producing sites. A number of big companies announced that this was exactly what they planned to do. French oil giant Total said that it planned to cut its proposed investment in the North Sea by £100 million. Shell has put £25 billion of investment into what it calls 'review' (which almost certainly means that they've cancelled it but don't like to say so). Other major oil companies have also said the high taxes make exploration in the North Sea too risky a proposition. (If an expensive search for oil results in a useable oil field the profits will mostly go to the Government. Would you bother? No, nor will they.)

The result is that the UK will need to import more gas than ever if citizens are to continue to heat their homes and cook their food. When the new levy was introduced the UK imported 50% of its gas. This came from Norway, Qatar (which we are supposed to regard with distaste because of its social policies and disapproval of homosexuality) and the United States of America which provides gas as Liquefied Natural Gas (LNG). The LNG travels across the Atlantic in large diesel fuelled tankers, and LNG produces eight times the carbon dioxide emissions produced by gas taken from the North Sea. More tankers are being built because the demand for LNG gas is so great.

And as if these new taxes weren't sufficiently discouraging, banks repeated that, having been pushed by climate change extremists, they would stop providing finance for oil companies wanting to look for oil.

The rules about not looking for new oil fields mean that OPEC, which currently provides a third of the world's oil, will soon provide half of the world's oil and will, inevitably, be incredibly powerful and able to set its prices for oil at whatever level it likes. It should be noted that OPEC is, entirely predictably and understandably, rather annoyed with the West for its unilateral declaration to stop using oil.

As if all this were not enough, the European Union independently introduced sanctions on Russian tankers, announcing that the only tankers allowed to access European ports, or to be serviced in European ports would be those which agreed to carry Russian oil at prices set by Europe. They also announced that tankers would not be allowed to buy insurance if they carried Russian oil on terms which the EU did not accept.

The result of this piece of lunacy was that Russia sells its oil to India and China (neither of which agreed to respect the oil price cap which the EU had unilaterally chosen) and that many of the world's tankers could no longer be hired to transport oil to European countries. And the end result of that was that the oil supply to Europe was cut still further and price went even higher.

Oh, and one other thing.

At the beginning of the winter of 2022 and 2023, gas tanks in Europe were still full of Russian gas which had been imported before the sanctions were introduced. These tanks will be empty by the start of the winter of 2023 and 2024.

The end result of all this will be that energy costs in Europe will probably be much higher in the winter of 2023-24 than in the winter of 2022-23 and, if the dispute with Russia continues, the costs will stay high and go higher indefinitely.

We have reached the end of cheap energy. The world's economy will be destroyed and millions of people will die because of this.

And the massive rise in the cost of oil and food which has resulted from all this will result in hundreds of millions dying in Africa and Asia because they cannot afford to buy oil or gas and, therefore, cannot afford to keep warm or to eat. These deaths (which appear not to have been noticed by the demonstrators who were busy pulling down the statues of heroes whom they regard as guilty of race crimes) will go a long way towards reducing the global population, as the conspirators have always planned.

And the valuable oil (which is running out) will be preserved so that the billionaires can use it to keep their super yachts moving and their expansive mansions and palaces well heated.

44.

For decades, the obvious way to provide sustainable electricity for a large and growing population has been to build nuclear power stations. Despite a couple of unrelated incidents (one at Chernobyl and the other in Japan) which had nothing to do with the inherent safety of nuclear power, just about every country in the world has eschewed nuclear power. The UK, in particular, has consistently rejected the idea of using nuclear power to provide electricity.

Nuclear power is very safe, it will work whatever the weather might be (unlike windmills which require wind and solar panels which won't work if there isn't any sunshine) and there is an ample supply or the essential uranium available at an unremarkable price.

And nuclear power stations don't need to be huge. It is possible to buy and erect small nuclear power stations (known as small modular reactors) which are pretty much the same as the nuclear power reactors used in submarines. These have been in use for decades. They are cost effective and require relatively little disruption or space. A small modular reactor will take up 25 acres of land whereas, in order to supply the same amount of energy, a solar farm would require 13,000 acres (of otherwise useful farmland) and wind turbines would require 32,000 acres (of otherwise useful farmland).

It would seem that there really isn't any sensible alternative to these.

But nuclear power has been consistently and defiantly rejected because the climate cultists don't approve of it.

Reactors take a long time to plan and to build and even if a government starts building nuclear reactors now they won't be finished and operational until the mid-2030s. The UK will be doomed to remain dependent upon imported gas until then – assuming that gas will be available to import.

And why don't the climate change cultists (a relatively small but vociferous body of professional campaigners comprising of woefully ignorant schoolgirls and 50-year-old unemployable zealots) approve of nuclear power?

Well, the only explanation is that nuclear power is efficient, effective, economical and safe. And now that the mad cultists have successfully banned fracking, nuclear power is pretty well the only game in town – unless we intend to import very environmentally unfriendly LNG for ever.

And the cultists and their masters want to see us all freeze or starve to death.

Incidentally, France the one country in the world which has for years now relied largely upon nuclear power for its electricity was unable to help the rest of Europe as the shortage of power in the autumn of 2022 became a real threat. France couldn't help because nearly half of its 56 reactors were suddenly offline for essential maintenance and repairs.

How curious, you might think, that a nation should arrange for nearly half of its reactors to be un-useable at the same time for essential maintenance and repairs.

And if you think that strange you should also know that there were serious threats that if and when the reactors were able to function again they would have to be closed down because of strikes.

45.

Two thirds of the British population support a referendum on whether the UK should continue on its disastrous journey towards net zero and it is clear that if such a referendum were held the plan would be abandoned.

Since Britain stopped using domestically sourced coal as a source of energy, the country has become dependent on imported gas, a product which is in short supply and likely to become increasingly expensive.

More and more people are aware that petrol and diesel powered cars will have to be abandoned by the mid-2030s at the latest despite the fact that electric cars have been proven to be worse for the environment than fossil fuelled cars. In addition it will be impossible to find enough copper, nickel, lithium and cobalt to build enough electric cars. The result (as planned) is that most members of the population will not own their own transport (other than bicycles or shoes)

46.

Mainstream media journalists frequently report that state pensioners in the UK receives £9,627.89 a year – or £185.15 a week.

This is, as you might expect, not exactly true.

Pensioners only receive this amount if they reached State pension age on or after 6th April 2016 and have paid at least 30 years' National Insurance contributions.

Anyone who reached the state pension age before that date, and who was, if male born before 6th April 1951 or, if female, born before 6th April 1953, will receive a state pension of £141.85 a week or £7,376.20 a year. They too must have paid at least 30 year's National insurance contributions.

That's a massive difference.

So, why do those who are older receive notably less pension income than pensioners who are younger?

I can only think of one possible explanation: because it is bloody impossible to pay for accommodation, food and heating fuel with an income of £7,376.20 a year.

I should know. That's my state pension.

The UK Government is deliberately discriminating against older pensioners – even though they have paid the same amount in National Insurance contributions.

When employment and private pensions are added to the state pension, the average pensioner has a gross income of £16,540.

Sadly, most people who have not yet reached retirement greatly over-estimate what they think their income will be. A recent survey showed that two thirds of Britons believe that will retire on an income of £21,730 a year. They are, I fear, going to be gravely disappointed.

47.

The European Union's policy is to reduce agricultural yields. This is being done to please climate change campaigners demanding that we move towards 'net zero', but the inevitable result is to reduce the amount of food available and to push up prices. It is important to understand that both these problems are a result of deliberate policies – particularly those introduced by the European Union.

In the UK, a major fertiliser producer closed one site permanently and suspended work at another because the cost of energy made fertiliser production uneconomical. The medium and long-term consequences of this will be a greater shortage of food and much higher prices.

The deliberately created food and fuel shortages are all part of the conspirators' ruthless, genocidal master plan. The designer war which we haven't quite declared against Russia now means that Western farmers are denied access to fertilisers – remember 28% of the global supply comes from Russia and Ukraine. That, on top of the soaring cost of fuel, and heavy handed Government action, means that thousands of farms are being closed as farmers just give up.

And, the Dutch Government, for example, just closed 3,000 working farms to please the cultists who claim they are worried we might have slightly better summers occasionally.

The absurd re-wilding schemes, whereby bison, boar, wolves, beavers and wild cats are introduced into the countryside, where they've never been before, are aimed at forcing people out of the countryside and into the towns as well as forcing food prices ever higher and ensuring that most people eat food made in laboratories. All those bison wandering around won't do fields of cabbages (or solar panels) much good.

People don't notice what is happening because they are misled by the distractions and mis-directions. The conspirators are like conjurors. They use feeble-minded, narcissistic exhibitionists like the self-obsessed Harry and Meghan to distract the feeble-minded masses. Fake rows about race and sexism are created to distract and divide. A word considered unsuitable becomes a life changing assault – but only if it goes one way. Meanwhile, racism against white males seems to continue unabated. A white man who applied for a job with West Yorkshire Police was apparently told that he wasn't suitable because they were hiring only women and ethnic minorities. Turn that around and see how it sounds. How many double woke lefties would start screaming if West Yorkshire Police were to announce that it wasn't recruiting women or non-white males? Or only recruiting non-Jews? Or only recruiting heterosexuals? The rhetoric about alleged race crimes has become absurd. Striking nurses protesting for more money carried posters complaining about a racist government. It was difficult to see what racism had to do with NHS staff pay since the NHS employs over 1.3 million people and there is no discrimination over pay. One look at the members of the Government would make nonsense of the accusation of racism. (I'm not supporting the Government, merely pointing out how every opportunity is used to bring race into every conversation.)

All this, it seems to me, is to create division, unhappiness and dissatisfaction – all designed to wreck communities and provide distraction from the far more important things which are happening.

48.

I've had my ID stolen and a bank account emptied so I know just how painful and expensive fraud can be. And I receive scores of clearly fraudulent emails every day. I doubt if I am alone. So I was annoyed to hear that the police in the UK no longer bother trying to catch fraudsters (who now make everyone's life a misery and who put us all at risk).

Fraud accounts for 39% of all crime but only 0.8% of police time is spent trying to catch fraudsters with the result that, according to a High Court judge called Clare Montgomery, 99% of fraud isn't even investigated. It seems that the police are more interested in tweeting and trawling the internet looking for politically incorrect remarks.

49.

The OECD has suggested a worldwide radical reform of property taxes. They want property valuations throughout the world to be regularly updated so that governments (or, more accurately I suspect, a future world government) can obtain the greatest amount of tax when a property is sold. Private homes, when sold, will not be exempt from taxation – as they are in the UK at the moment. It is recommended that there should also be regular, national taxes based on the value of property or land. These taxes will be separate and in addition to local property and land taxes.

50.

Growth is dependent upon productivity. If a nation does not produce more goods, or provide more services, there will be no growth and the constantly increasingly standard of living which everyone expects will come to a grinding halt. (The unasked question is: why should everyone expect their standard of living to rise every year?)

The problem is that productivity is falling.

Terrible production figures (particularly in the UK, where production is probably lower than anywhere in the known world) are invariably blamed on some very odd causes.

In the UK, for example, most politicians and journalists blame Brexit – the universal culprit and easy-to-blame cause for every problem imaginable.

But Brexit has absolutely nothing to do with the UK's low productivity.

There are several causes.

First, high unemployment. The official unemployment figures are no higher than usual but these are, inevitably, misleading. The fact is that in the UK there are now millions of people who should be working but who have decided not to bother. The latest official UK Government figures (in late 2022) show that there are nine million people, aged 16-64, who are what is officially, and politely, known as 'economically inactive'. These people fall into several categories. There are those who are genuinely ill and who are waiting to be seen and treated in the health service. (Good luck with that for the last time I looked there were over ten million Britons waiting for essential medical treatment. And that figure rises daily.) Around the world tens of millions of people now claim to be unable to work because of long covid – an imaginary disease which has been promoted by politicians and the media because it's convenient and useful for the conspirators. There are those who enjoyed the furlough years (when taxpayers gave them huge amounts of money to stay at home and watch television) so much that they have chosen to stay at home for the rest of their lives, popping out only to slip into the supermarket to collect another six or twelve pack of beer. And there are the young people who have never worked, and who have decided that they don't like the look of it because it doesn't look much fun so they don't intend to bother. Instead they intend to follow a life of cut price hedonism at the expense of the long-suffering taxpayers. Nine million Britons of working age are not working or looking for work. They may or may not have tried it but they are tired of work. Sunak's free money has encouraged them to believe that work is for other people. Massive rises in benefits payments are part of the plan to make everyone dependent upon the Government. Why work when the Government will give you more money to stay at home and watch television or play computer games? Millions of young people are at university studying courses in subjects that are of no value whatsoever and which will lead them into debt, long covid and a life on benefits.

Second, high levels of immigration (particularly illegal immigration). Immigration is usually regarded as boosting productivity but it doesn't. Productivity levels are measured by the amount of 'somethings' that a nation produces per person. (The 'somethings' vary from industry to industry. In the car industry the 'somethings' are motor cars produced. In the health care industry the 'somethings' are operations performed, patients treated or whatever.) The problem with immigrants is that many of them don't contribute at all. Indeed, they cost a great deal of money in housing, benefits and bureaucracy. The conspirators and the collaborators usually claim that more immigration is a solution to productivity problems. They say this because immigration has important socio-political purposes which have a great deal to do with destroying a nation's culture and economy but nothing whatsoever to do with productivity.

Third, there is the problem caused by the number of people who insist on staying at home to work even though there is clear evidence that people who work from home (when they should be working in an office) will do a shoddy job and spend most of their time playing games, chatting to their neighbours, amusing the baby or the dog or messing around on the internet. An astonishing 20% of males are happy to go to work in order to work (and earn their pay cheque). The figure for women is much worse, with only 10% of female employees being willingly prepared to go to work. The rest insist on staying at home – usually announcing that they need to be at home with their children (as though they have, for the first time, discovered that they have family responsibilities which didn't exist when they applied for their job). The greatest lunacy is that the NHS is now allowing all menopausal members of staff to work from home if they feel they would like to. The chaos at the UK Passport Office appears to have been largely caused by the fact that many people supposedly employed there were working from home. And despite being ordered to go to work, many civil servants are still refusing to do so. Why they haven't been fired is a mystery. Applicants for a recently advertised job nearly all insisted that they must be allowed to work at home whenever they wanted to. The job was for a position working in a gym.

Fourth, there is the problem caused by a shortage of essential parts and so on – itself caused by absurd working practices and endless, restrictive legislation. In Germany, Volkswagen announced at the end of 2022 that it had 150,000 unfinished cars because of problems with their suppliers. Productivity problems are not unique to the UK, though they are worse there than anywhere else. Growth rates and productivity have both declined in America and both are going backwards.

Fifth, women (and men) who become parents are entitled to take a year off work. And many happily do. It is utterly absurd that a man should be allowed to take parental leave every time he becomes a father or indeed that a new mother should be allowed to take twelve months away from work every time she has a baby. She cannot be replaced while she is away and small businesses find this an intolerable burden.

Sixth, Government legislation means it is now legally necessary for employers to allow employees to enjoy what is called flexible working or flexitime. This lunacy means that employees can work when they feel like working. So, for example, shop workers might decide that they would find their work less demanding if they came in to work between midnight and eight in the morning when there are fewer annoying customers around. Please don't laugh. When I ran a publishing business, one member of staff demanded to be allowed to work over Christmas when there was absolutely nothing to do because there were no orders coming in and so no books to be sent out. This is the sort of legislation which shows that legislators have never run a business or had to meet a payroll. It is also the sort of legislation which shows just how determined the conspirators are to destroy everything.

Seventh, the officially endorsed introduction of the four day working week has proved popular with people who don't like having to work five days a week. And it has already begun to devastate businesses and service industries. Health care, for example, has been thrown into turmoil now that GPs are working an average of 26 hours a week and are demanding that their working 'week' be reduced to 21 hours. Evidence obtained by examining (anonymous) mobile phone data shows that a massive number of people who are allegedly part of the working population now work only from Tuesday to Thursday (which is now, unofficially, the working week). The evidence shows that activity at seaside towns and inland resorts is as high on Fridays and Mondays as at the traditional weekend of Saturday and Sunday.

Eighth, the failure of the educational system. Since schools closed (for absolutely no good reason) during the fake pandemic, the incidence of illiteracy and innumeracy have soared. And children leave school with no sense of what work entails or what responsibility means. Education fell apart when schools started telling children the questions they'd be getting in their exams.

All things considered, it is not surprising that productivity is at an all-time low. And it's going to get consistently worse. Growth will stay low or even negative. Huge imports (of oil and gas for example) will mean that costs soar, inflation soars and interest rates stay high.

Remember the mantra of those promoting the Great Reset: 'You will own nothing'.

51.

Low and negative interest rates pushed everyone (including private investors running their own portfolios, and professional investors running investment funds and pension companies) into investing in risky assets in the hope that they would be able to earn some money through high capital gains or huge dividends to help them avoid inevitable losses due to even modest inflation rates. Risky investments often fail and those who put their money into them often lose some or all of their money.

This was all part of the plan to impoverish those who had a little money saved for their later years.

52.

If global warming ever becomes a reality, instead of a convenient myth used to excuse a growing dictatorship, we should welcome it.

Energy prices are never going back down.

Oil is in increasingly short supply and it is going to become ever more expensive to heat homes, offices, shops and public buildings.

During this winter, around 100,000 elderly citizens are going to die of the cold in the UK alone. This, of course, is exactly what the conspirators want. Most are going to die because they cannot afford to keep warm. Throughout the world there will be millions of deaths due to the cost of heating.

53.

Recessions always lead to despair, ill health, anger and eventually to extreme policies. A minute drop in incomes or in employment will always, inevitably, lead to massively increased mortality rates.

54.

As food and fuel become increasingly scarce there seems little doubt that rationing will be introduced.

Governments will use the rationing process as part of their social credit programme. They will only allow citizens to purchase food or fuel with digital money (and not with cash), they will only allow those who have had the 'recommended' vaccinations to purchase essentials and they will limit the sale of specific items to those with suitable apps on their smart phones.

55.

The majority of journalists and some members of the public tend to regard the peer review system as a vital part of the scientific process.

If a new piece of research is published they will dismiss it as worthless if it hasn't been 'peer reviewed'.

I've got bad news for them.

The peer review system is not just worthless – it is dangerous and designed to perpetuate errors, misconceptions and faulty reasoning.

The problem is that the 'peers' who are chosen to 'review' a scientific paper or a piece of scientific research will invariably be members of a small group of individuals who are committed to supporting the establishment – and who almost certainly have financial links to the establishment. If they are peer reviewing a medical paper they will, in 99 times out of 100, have links to the pharmaceutical industry.

Scientists who are asked to review a piece of research will be part of the system they are reviewing. They will depend for their livelihood on reputations built on supporting the establishment. The scientist who doesn't do what he is expected to do, and who welcomes original thinking, will soon be exiled and find himself unemployable. His work won't be published in the standard journals.

A scientist who questions accepted beliefs (however blatantly wrong they may be) will not be asked to 'peer review' anything.

And the problem, of course, is that the pharmaceutical industry is known to be riddled with corrupt people and corrupt practices.

Scientific research which is original, and of real value, will be suppressed if it is considered to be inconvenient to the pharmaceutical industry and/or the medical establishment.

There is no doubt that the peer review system will be used to suppress valuable new ideas and essential truths.

It is, for example, largely because of the peer review system that valuable, valid information about covid-19 and the vaccination programmes currently being promoted, is demonised by the media and the public.

It is thanks to the peer review system that four out of ten patients given drugs suffer side effects (some lethal) and why one in six hospital patients has been made ill by doctors. It is thanks to the peer review system that scores of allegedly thoroughly tested drugs have had to be withdrawn.

In a world where truth was of importance, the peer review system would be regarded as worthless and discredited; it is corrupt and serves merely to maintain the lies promoted by the medical establishment – which is, of course, owned by the pharmaceutical industry.

56.

Freedom of speech is disappearing globally.

Indonesia's parliament has ratified laws that will forbid sex outside marriage, cohabitation of unmarried couples and insulting the president and state institutions. The laws will apply to foreigners, including holiday makers.

I don't care that the law forbids sex outside marriage or that it prohibits cohabitation (those who want to enjoy such fruits can and will leave Indonesia) but I care very much that Indonesia will be another country where it is illegal to criticise the establishment.

57.

The UK tax code now consists of 16,000 pages and very few accountants or tax inspectors understand it. Moreover, tax inspectors frequently make elementary but devastating errors because they don't understand their own regulations. And it is no surprise that these errors seem inevitably to be the disadvantage of taxpayers.

Taxes have been deliberately raised so high that it is now almost impossible for anyone to become rich. The Government lies about it but there are many people in Britain now paying 60-70% of their earnings to the taxman. That's not much of an incentive to work, of course. As they know. Taxes in the UK are as high as they were in World War II and they are going to go higher. Windfall taxes on oil companies are stopping exploration for more oil and they're further damaging pension funds which were devastated, and in some cases cut in half, by Truss and Kwarteng's unusual budget. (Curiously, by the way, much of the damage occurred when officials of the International Monetary Fund took the unprecedented step of criticising that budget. It was the IMF's intervention which contributed to the rise in UK borrowing costs. Cowardly IMF officials later refused to appear before a House of Commons committee to explain their actions.)

As a result, thousands of the people paying high taxes are leaving the UK and they're being replaced by hundreds of thousands of immigrants who will cost the country a fortune in housing and benefits. The only people supporting unlimited immigration are the people who aren't paying for it. Other European countries won't take Albanians – why should they, they're not oppressed – but at the present rate it won't be long before there are more young Albanian men living in England than there are living in Albania.

And those taxpayers who are paying 40% tax are also paying 20% VAT, fuel taxes, stamp duties, and on and on. Destroying the middle classes is an integral part of the conspirators' plan. The State today is 50% bigger than it was under war criminal Tony Blair. There are millions of job vacancies and yet there are many millions of healthy people claiming benefits – in not a few cases because they enjoyed the furlough months and have been struck down with an imaginary disease called long covid.

Taxes are high because Britons are living in a kleptocracy. An astonishing £12 billion was wasted on defective or overpriced PPE. Chums of Government ministers were looting the country, and a king's ransom was wasted on gloves and masks which were useless and had to be thrown away. To make matters worse, the UK Government is now spending £7 billion on equality and diversity measures – left wing spend, spend policies designed to create division rather than to heal it. And of course they're wasting over £100 billion on a railway line that no one wants.

All this means that ambitions are being deliberately thwarted, with the result that people become frustrated and dissatisfied. It has become impossible for anyone to rise above their upbringing (a classical ambition which is most prevalent in Britain). The rich can get richer but that is all.

Incidentally, in his ill-fated budget in the early autumn of 2022, Kwasi Kwarteng removed the cap on bankers' bonuses. This was the only aspect of his budget which survived when Jeremy Hunt introduced his budget a few weeks later – showing without much doubt that the aim of the Government in the UK was to help the very rich (investment bankers) to escape the clampdown designed to stop 'ordinary' people from saving or satisfying their modest ambitions.

The billionaires will become trillionaires and the middle classes (and the aspiring middle classes) will be systematically and deliberately destroyed.

The hidden truth in all this is that economists, politicians and civil servants at the Treasury know that the best way to increase a government's income is to reduce taxes. The UK Treasury's own analysis proved this. (See the UK Treasury's own 'Growth Plan 2022 Blue Book'.) Increasing taxes isn't being done to improve the Government's income but to impoverish the people.

High new taxes are discouraging businesses from investing in new machinery or new premises. The UK Government has put up corporation tax from 19% to 25% and companies are frightened that the politicians will also invent new windfall taxes (such as the windfall tax which has taken the tax on oil companies to 75%.)

There's something else too.

During 2022 there was much talk of 'quiet quitting' – which simply meant that employees who had enjoyed the furlough times had decided that they weren't going to do anything other than the bare bones of their work. They wouldn't try harder, they wouldn't do overtime and they wouldn't go the extra mile (as the cliché has it).

Well, high taxes and 'quiet quitting' have resulted in companies now introducing 'quiet firing'. A growing number of firms who want to get rid of useless employees are forcing people out by creating a hostile environment which encourages them to leave early by themselves. The boss doesn't talk to them. They are encouraged to work from home. They get all the dull jobs and are treated as junior members of staff. And they don't get the pay rise they rather hoped for.

58.

Attitudes towards work seem to have changed dramatically in the last few years.

The millennials (aka snowflakes) seemed bad enough. Their curious and in-built sense of entitlement and self-regard meant that they were constantly disappointed; frustrated by a world which failed to give them everything they wanted the very moment they announced that they wanted it.

Their successors, generation z, are infinitely worse.

If they condescend to accept employment (and they do the interviewing and expect to make the decision about whether or not the job will be theirs) they make sure everyone realises that their work-life balance is crucial. They expect to be able to work from home and to choose precisely when they work and what they do. If they really have to attend an office they expect free gym membership, long holidays, sabbaticals and free cakes and drinks all day long. They want therapists available to deal with their mental and physical ills and they insist on being respected and valued by their bosses. They want free yoga sessions, free meals and a meditation room where they can relax and get away from it if they feel the slightest bit of stress coming on. They expect to be allowed to take their pets into the office with them. Many have the sort of sense of entitlement and self-regard as has been exhibited by the king of England's younger son.

They are, in short, lazy and selfish little bastards and they are part of the reason why our very future is in peril.

59.

When it was reported that inflation in the UK had hit double figures, public services were devastated by a series of strikes led by unions which insisted that their members had been hard done by and deserved huge pay rises. It was no coincidence that everyone seemed to be going on strike at once. Doctors, nurses, midwives, firemen, train drivers, ambulance drivers, postmen, civil servants, port workers, airport workers and millions more went on strike. Doctors wanted a 21 hour week and a 30% pay rise. Nurses ('your money or your life') were threatening to refuse to deal with emergencies or cancer patients and said they would settle for a more modest 19.2%. Junior doctors demanded a pay rise of 26%. (Both nurses and junior doctors were in pay grades leading to annual salaries of £60,000.)

This was not a uniquely British phenomenon, by the way. Railway workers and nurses were, at the same time, also on strike within the EU.

Strikes, particularly those involving government employees working in the health service, were carefully coordinated in order to cause most disruption (and, therefore, cause most pain and suffering to patients and, presumably, to kill as many innocents as possible). It is difficult to avoid the feeling that the strikes were designed to destroy the NHS, break down society (ready for the Great Reset) and wreck the economy.

What no one in the media bothered to mention was that state employees in the UK have massively better pensions than the pensions enjoyed by private sector employees. The public service pensions are guaranteed by the Government (which means by tax payers) and when pensions are taken into account, it was clear that public sector workers are 6% better off than private sector workers.

Railway workers (technically employed by private companies) had in recent years been heavily subsidised by taxpayers and with salaries of £60,000 could hardly claim to be underpaid. They had, however, rejected a pay offer of 8-9% together with valuable perks. The strikes were destroying the railways (people were staying at home or finding some other way to travel) and it is difficult to believe this wasn't part of a deliberate plan to destroy the wider economy and stop people travelling.

As an aside it is not difficult to argue that unions and strikes are now as outdated as buggy whips. In the West, workers are not now abused as they were in the days when unions were first created. There is considerable need for unions in Asia, of course, but the unions aren't much in evidence there.

Union leaders seem not to realise (or, perhaps, care) that our society is much more complex than it used to be and that we are now all dependent upon one another. Strikes do massive and sometimes permanent damage, and it is our inter-dependence which gives unions their unprecedented and dangerous powers. Since policemen and soldiers are not allowed to strike it seems absurd, or even obscene, to allow health care workers, refuse workers, teachers and transport workers to strike.

The motives of the unions can perhaps be judged that in January 2023, when the UK Government announced new legislation to enforce minimum levels of service in eight sectors (including the National Health Service) the Trades Union Congress warned that unions would 'fight every step of the way' to scupper the legislation which was aimed to ensure that public services (such as health care) functioned adequately during strikes. It is scarcely believable that anyone would oppose such eminently and essential humanitarian legislation. But the unions declared that they would.

In comparison, after a life-time of paying taxes and national insurance payments, I receive a full state pension of £7,436 – the standard pension for a 76-year-old.

The economy (what's left of it) will be destroyed if all these strikers get what they are demanding. Small businesses and the self-employed (none of whom can put up their prices by 19.2%) will be devastated. Inflation is hitting everyone not just people in public service jobs.

60.

'The factory of the future will have only two employees: a man and a dog. The man will be there to feed the dog. The dog will be there to keep the man from touching the equipment.'
Management guru Warren Bennis

61.

New postage stamps are being introduced in the UK. These contain scannable bar codes. When these were introduced, people holding stamps which did not contain scannable bar codes were left holding worthless pieces of paper and although they were told that they could exchange their worthless stamps for the new ones, there seems no doubt that Royal Mail will have made millions by this change.

The ultimate, long-term aim is, it seems to me, to enable the Royal Mail to scan every letter at every stage of its journey so that the sender and recipient can be identified.

The authorities, able to read private emails, have for some time been worried by the fact that what is known as 'snail mail' provides people with a way to communicate privately.

Up until January 2023, Britons could use all their old unused stamps quite legally. If you had a mint penny black and you were foolish enough to want to do so, you could put the stamp on an envelope as part of your postage. No more. Mint stamps are now worth only what a collector will pay for them.

62.

It is impossible for citizens to defend themselves against the predatory activities of a thousand corporate and institutional Big Brothers

There are so many closed circuit television cameras in London (the most intrusive city after Monaco) that if you are not in your own home, or inside someone else's home, you are probably being watched.

Actually, if you are at home and within twenty feet of a television set, a computer or a smart phone (whether or not the item is switched on) you are probably being either watched or listened to or both.

And if the cameras don't get you, the snitches will for governments everywhere are encouraging citizens to reveal whatever they know about their neighbours to the authorities (usually referred to as 'the proper authorities').

This is part of the process known as 'social credit.

63.

Stagflation means low growth (stagnant economies) and high inflation. We're going to see a lot of this word in the next year or two. It's as nasty as shingles and much longer lasting.

64.

Governments all around the world are now irredeemably statist. This is no accident. Politicians have been pushed by the conspirators (who control them) into believing that bailouts, protectionism and hand-outs are essential government policies.

Every government in the world is moving further and further to the left. In the US, Biden's Democratic Party has been taken over by left wing extremists. In the UK, Johnson and Sunak have presided over the most left wing government in British history. The conservative party should rename itself the communist party mark II.

It would make sense (and be popular) for governments to control immigration, reform planning regulations, embrace free trade, remove absurd and unnecessary regulations and reduce taxes.

But they will do none of these things because they are not things that the conspirators want them to do.

65.

Everyone who does anything independently must these days expect to be reviewed and rated. Authors, musicians, plumbers, café owners, hoteliers and shop keepers live or die by the reviews they receive from their customers. Sadly, it is common for artists or businesses to be destroyed by ruthlessly critical reviews posted by commercial rivals or, simply, by those who, for one reason or another, disagree with something the artist or business owner has done or said.

I believe that this new trend has two specific purposes.

First, it is to prepare us for social credit – whereby we will all be constantly reviewed by society and other citizens in a more than a hundred different ways.

Second, the review system is deliberately designed to get rid of troublesome campaigners and to destroy small businesses which might otherwise prove to be a nuisance as far as big businesses are concerned. Big companies can and do hire professional staff to manage the comments on sites where reviews are published. They can instruct their staff to write glowing reviews, they can arrange for the deletion of potentially damaging reviews and they can pay for good reviews to be published by the thousand. Small business owners, already stressed and over-worked, don't have the time or the funds to do any of that. Many independently managed cafes, pubs, hotels and shops have been destroyed by campaigns of negative ratings.

66.

The tenth man rules means that if there are ten people in a meeting, and nine of them agree on one thing, then it is the duty of the tenth man to disagree with the consensus. The idea is that any concept which appears to garner universal support (and which is regarded as inevitably correct because the majority agree with it) should be questioned by someone.

Once the fake covid pandemic (and all its frightening consequences) had been given world-wide approval, there was no debate and no questioning. There was no respect for the tenth man rule.

As I discovered to my personal cost, anyone who questioned the approved consensus, was immediately demonised, lied about and dismissed as dangerous and irrelevant. There was no debate (the BBC, remember, even said that no one who questioned vaccination would be allowed onto any of its programmes even if they were right) and anyone who tried to publish facts which did not fit neatly into the official viewpoint was oppressed, suppressed and silenced. YouTube, for example, deleted any video which carried information which did not fit into the officially approved propaganda – even if the information deleted was provably accurate and offered by an experienced health professional. Time and time again my videos were removed because they contained simple truths which were considered too accurate to be acceptable. I was refused entry to social media sites because I did not pander to the official line. I became a non-person, and I was lied about and demonised on the mainstream media and on social media. I was expelled from the Royal Society of Arts because I had told the truth. It was repeatedly claimed that I had no medical qualifications even though the evidence that I had been a registered and licensed GP was easy to find. And, of course, there has been a regular and plentiful supply of abuse (usually anonymous) and the usual death threats (always anonymous). Three years ago I had a good, solid reputation. My books were regularly reviewed. Today, I even have to use a pseudonym with workmen. All I've ever done is tell the truth (and to provide evidence proving that I was telling the truth) but I feel like an outlaw.

67.

In order to make covid-19 appear more important than the flu, journalists have invariably used the initial capital to make covid look special and important. What journalist would write of Flu rather than flu?

Worse still, some journalists and editors insist on referring to covid as COVID. Indeed, many search engines automatically correct anyone who dares to write covid in lower case.

68.

You'd have to be really stupid (as, I'm afraid, it is clear that most of the population is) to think that the destruction of health care was anything other than deliberate.

Look, specifically, at what has happened in the UK.

The authorities destroyed general practice by training far more female GPs than male GPs (knowing that most of them would want to work part-time). Then they did more damage by allowing GPs to work librarian hours and to abandon evening, night, weekend and bank holiday calls. Then they allowed GPs to stop seeing patients at all – allowing them to attempt to make diagnoses over the telephone (proven to be deadly dangerous) or via a video link (dodgy at the best of times, always dangerous and not available to a large chunk of the population). Destroying general practice put extra pressure on accident and emergency departments and on the ambulance service (who else are you going to turn to on a Sunday afternoon or at 3am in the morning when you are seriously in need of medical advice?).

The effective closure of general practice fitted in nicely with the advent of telemedicine whereby GPs who had cut their working week to 26 hours or less could offer advice over the internet to other doctors' patients – and get huge additional fees for doing so.

All this was made considerably worse by bizarre and completely irrational new regulations about social distancing and masks which gave GPs an excuse to close their practices and to 'see' patients only over the telephone.

Lockdowns were always useless and always dangerous. Masks were always useless and always dangerous. The fact that hospital staff are still wearing them, and expecting patients and relatives to wear them, is proof that those who are masked are completely uninterested in medical science and only interested in compliance. They have abandoned patients and medicine and become enforcers for a thoroughly corrupt system. My small book *Proof that face masks do more harm than good* took three years to find a publisher. It contains all the evidence anyone needs – proving that masks don't work but do kill.

Social distancing was always useless and always dangerous and mentally disturbing. Long covid never existed – though around the world millions of hypochondriacs and idlers are now permanently off work because of it, and being subsidised by the rapidly falling few who are still working. When the UK Government put up benefits by more than 10% they pretty well ensured that wages would soar that much; that the self-employed and small businesses would be destroyed and that inflation would stay dangerously high.

Everything has been designed to make the weak-willed and feeble-minded afraid and compliant. Government committees admitted that their aim was to create fear out of nothing. Governments have been deliberately using fear for a long time because they were advised by their brainwashing specialists that it works.

The aim, as I've been telling you since early 2020, was to destroy the health service and destroy the economy, to damage immune systems – particularly among the very old and the very young who are the ones they want to kill first – to create depression, to push up interest rates, to push up inflation and to kill people with the cold and soaring food prices. It's all there in videos I made in early 2020. Incidentally, after several attempts at publishing were banned, there is now a published collection of those scripts called *Covid-19: The Greatest Hoax in History*. Even if the videos are gone – and some of them have been repeatedly and deliberately banned – the transcripts are still available.

Early in 2023, it was clear that governments were, as predicted, making a real effort to persuade people to start wearing masks again. Every mainstream photograph taken in a hospital showed everyone wearing masks. Politicians started demanding that masks be worn in public places.

Utterly absurd claims were made for the expected number of deaths from the 2020 version of the flu. Those making predictions seemed unaware that according to the World Health Organisation it was not unknown for 650,000 people a year to die from the standard annual flu, worldwide, during a six month flu season. Later the authorities seemed equally unaware that the Government's own statistics had shown that covid-19 had actually killed fewer people than the flu. And no one seemed to care that according to the World Health Organisation more than eight million people a year are believed to die from the direct use of tobacco and from second-hand exposure to tobacco smoke. The scare-mongering figures promoted as a possible outcome from the fake pandemic were far still behind the number of deaths from other, existing infectious diseases. It is important to remember that the World Health Organisation (which officially represents the world's countries plus Bill Gates, who seems to have given himself national status) is using its Pandemic Treaty and its International Health Regulations Review Committee to give itself massive powers over every citizen in the world.

At the end of 2022, the UK Government launched a new scare campaign and again encouraged people to snitch on friends, relatives and neighbours who have log fires so that they can eat and keep warm on the same day. It was officially announced that polluted air could kill as many people as covid. (I hate snitching and sneaking – it's a way the evil ones are recruiting collaborators.) Well, the Government was actually telling the truth for once. Polluted air kills around 30,000 people a year in Britain. And that is actually rather more than were killed by covid-19. It's also the same as the number who die each year from the flu – and less than some years. In 2017-2018, for example, the UK Government reported that 50,100 deaths were due to the flu in a four month period. This is far more than the Government claims were killed by covid-19.

The so-called opinion makers now admit that covid-19 is symptomatically similar to colds and the flu. That's exactly what the British Government's advisors said in March 2020. Everyone who has said differently has lied.

You'll remember that when covid-19 was being promoted like a rock star on tour, everyone around the world talked about nothing else. Every third rate scientist and Z list celebrity in the world shared their inexpert conviction that covid-19 was the new plague. Meanwhile, the traditional flu disappeared completely. And you will have noticed that the flu is now back. Indeed, the UK Government is warning that the flu could kill 30,000 people this flu season. That's pretty normal. And the odd thing is that covid-19 is no longer going to kill 30,000. It seems to have disappeared.

You don't need many brain cells to see the pattern. Flu kills 30,000 in the UK. Then, when it disappears and, covid-19 kills 30,000. Then covid-19 is replaced by a new version of the flu which will, we are told, kill 30,000 in the UK in 2022-2023. There is, of course, a new and inadequately tested flu jab available for those whose only discernible skill is in rolling up their sleeves.

Right from the start, of course, I've been telling my readers that covid-19 was simply the rebranded flu. And what a miracle it was that this edition of the flu suddenly appeared overnight in every country in the world. Not even with aeroplane travel has any other infection ever spread so quickly and so thoroughly.

I mentioned a few dozen times that the toxic, inadequately tested, ineffective and dangerous covid jab would kill more than covid-19 itself. The figures have pretty well proved that to be true.

In 2020, I listed the side effects of the covid-19 jab, including myocarditis, heart attacks, strokes and clots. Since then masses of evidence has accumulated showing that the warning was accurate.

A study in Thailand showed that 30% of young adults have had cardiovascular injuries. Doctors ignored the evidence.

In 2020 and 2021, I also published evidence showing that there would be brain damage. And now there are experts who believe that the brains of those who have been jabbed are damaged – in much the same way that brains are damaged after lobotomies. The personality changes we are seeing are real. The internet is awash with peer reviewed studies which prove that the jabs should have never been given to anyone. But ignorant and dangerous doctors are ignoring the evidence and continuing to instruct nurses to kill and injure their patients for big fees.

Everything else they told us was also a lie.

The PCR test was always useless and always dangerous. In the UK, thanks to a politician called Matt Hancock, who should be locked in a four foot square cell eating cockroaches, the test and trace scheme is recognised to have been a complete waste of £37 billion of taxpayers' money. Experts were paid £1,000 a day to provide advice.

Hospitals were destroyed by administrators who insisted that all members of staff should practice social distancing (an arbitrary social nonsense with no scientific support whatsoever) and wear masks at all times (proven to be useless and damaging) and insist on everyone (staff and patients) taking PCR tests (proven to be entirely useless) and having inadequately tested covid-19 jabs (proven beyond any doubt to be ineffective and dangerous). Positive PCR tests were used to give hospital staff an excuse to stay at home and to close wards and outpatient departments (thereby further extending waiting lists and helping to destroy the already worthless National Health Service). Even at the beginning of 2023, hospitals and doctors were still performing and relying on PCR tests even though all the evidence available showed that they were of absolutely no value. Worse still, when a patient had a positive PCR test they were immediately diagnosed as suffering from covid-19 and any other, more serious and genuine disorders, were often left ignored and untreated.

It is clear that there was a significant hidden agenda in the promotion of the utterly useless PCR tests. Companies made huge fortunes (measured in billions) from tests which didn't work (and which were never truly expected to work, but which were used to confine and imprison healthy people). Those companies are now promoting a variety of health tests which are sold at home. Those who purchase the tests can then obtain an analysis from the seller. This is clearly a plan for the future – and a plan that will fit in with telemedicine, whereby patients will obtain health care from computers (with chat-bot robots asking the questions and providing the answers). People who have chronic diseases will be able to test themselves regularly and people who have no symptoms will be able to obtain diagnoses by testing themselves. They will then, presumably, also be able to treat themselves. The absurdly useless PCR tests have accustomed millions to tests which they perform themselves or which are performed by a lay person (rather than a doctor or even a nurse).

The jabs were endorsed by celebrities and royals (most of whom knew virtually nothing about the jab they were recommending) and given by doctors and nurses (most of whom also knew virtually nothing about the jab they were recommending). Today, the covid-19 jabs are widely recognised among independent medically qualified professionals to be untested and dangerous. It is also generally accepted that they should have never been rolled out to billions of patients without much more testing – and that if they had been properly tested they would have never been used on more than the handful of patients involved in early testing.

There is now no doubt whatsoever that doctors who gave the experimental jab to their patients without explaining to them that they were being given a relatively untested drug (which had not been proved to work or to be safe) were breaking the Hippocratic Oath, the Nuremberg Code of Conduct and the Helsinki Declaration. All the doctors (and nurses) who gave the covid-19 jab should be arrested and lose their licences to practice. Just how many of these health care professionals are psychopaths and how many are simply greedy and uncaring is a moot point.

By the end of 2022, even the British Government was admitting that the weekly death rate in the UK was much higher than it had been even during the alleged covid-19 pandemic. Government figures showed that on average an additional 800 people a week were dying. The Government blamed this on the fact that patients had been unwilling to visit their doctors because they knew there were busy. There was no mention of the fact that most GPs were still refusing to see patients (even during the 26 hours a week that they were supposed to be working). There was no mention of the fact that over ten million people were on waiting lists for treatment because of the lockdowns and the closure of many hospital departments.

And, most significant of all, there was absolutely no mention of the fact that the covid-19 jabs were known to be killing thousands of people who had previously been perfectly healthy. So many children were suddenly dropping dead with previously non-existent heart trouble that defibrillators were fitted in schools. So many healthy adults (including professional sports players) were dropping dead that doctors attempting to explain the phenomenon (known as Sudden Adult Death Syndrome) blamed absolutely everything they could think of except the one obvious cause – the dangerous 'vaccine' that was the one common factor. In the US alone, over 270 professional athletes and former professional athletes died of cardiac arrest after being jabbed with the covid-19 experimental 'vaccine' – a jab which, we should always remember, does not do what it was said to do and is not as safe as was promised. More lies have been told about this medication than about all other drugs and vaccines in history.

The danger of the so-called 'vaccine' was so widely recognised among members of the public that many were refusing to accept blood transfusions from donors who had been given the covid-19 jab. Numerous parents asked that their babies not be given 'contaminated' blood but in several countries such requests were greeted angrily by doctors. Despite the fact that at least one baby died after being given 'contaminated' blood, doctors threatened to remove babies and small children from their parents if they even asked for 'clean' blood to be given. In at least one case a child was removed from its parents because such a request was made.

I had first warned about the specific dangers of the covid-19 jabs back in 2020 but throughout 2021 and 2022, the evidence about the dangers accumulated at a startling rate. So, for example, a paper published in the Journal of Medical Ethics (itself published as one of the British Medical Journals) described how students at North American universities risked dis-enrolment (which I assume means that they would be thrown out) if they were unvaccinated. The authors concluded that 'University booster mandates are unethical because they: 1) are not based on an updated (Omicron era) stratified risk-benefit assessment for this age group; 2) may result in a net harm to healthy young adults; 3) are not proportionate: expected harms are not outweighed by public health benefits given modest and transient effectiveness of vaccines against transmission; 4) violate the reciprocity principle because serious vaccine-related harms are not reliably compensated due to gaps in vaccine injury schemes; and 5) may result in wider social harms.'

Insurance companies refused to pay out when people died after being 'vaccinated', claiming that such deaths were properly classified as suicide. And, of course, governments had, at the request of software billionaire and vaccine investor Bill Gates, given the manufacturing drug companies indemnity so that they could not be sued. Governments made relatively small payments to those injured by the covid-19 jabs (or to the relatives of victims who had died) but these were woefully inadequate.

Tragically, the medical establishment and the media have silenced and demonised independent doctors (probably because they realise that they are now too far into the fraud to admit that it was a fraud and a dangerous if profitable one). I am reminded of the economist John Maynard Keynes who, when confronted by a critic who accused him of having changed his mind, responded: 'When the facts change, I change my mind. What do you do?'

It seems that the medical establishment, the Government advisors, the media doctors and journalists in general all prefer to stick to the lies they told at the beginning of the fraud, and which have been responsible for untold thousands of deaths and injuries.

The destruction of hospital services (with patients having to wait months for essential tests) has enabled health care companies to develop home testing programmes for a wide range or disorders (including heart disease and cancer) so that patients can make their own diagnoses at home without bothering a doctor or hospital. We are being taken along a road which leads directly to what is called telemedicine – with patients testing themselves, accessing their investigation results directly, making diagnostic decisions themselves and, if they're lucky, being treated by doctors at the other end of a telephone or an internet link. 'Proper' medicine, as has been practised for generations is over. When my wife needed an operation for her breast cancer, the essential pre-med examination, to confirm that she was fit for surgery and had no heart or blood pressure problems, was conducted entirely over the telephone.

Health care as we used to know it has been deliberately destroyed and the socialist NHS in the UK (with its 1.3 million employees and a virtual monopoly on health care as far as most people are concerned) is a perfect testing ground for this new type of health care. But precisely the same changes are being made everywhere, in every country in the world. Health care is being deliberately destroyed, taken apart piece by piece, to protect us from non-existent global warming and to prepare us for the Great Reset where those of us remaining will be regarded and treated as drones. Destroying health care will have the added advantage that it will result in a massive number of deaths and reduce the size of the world's population – for long an aim of the conspirators within the cabal.

69.

It will not be long before patients are being invited and encouraged to treat themselves with remedies, solutions and even operations selected from a smorgasbord of available options offered online. If you think I am joking you should look back at what has already happened (much of which I predicted) and ask yourself whether you think anything is now impossible.

The medical establishment has already announced that fewer patients should be tested or treated because of the threat of (non-existent) global warming. There was never a shred of evidence that this was a sensible policy but it was immediately adopted by hospitals and doctors everywhere. Doctors writing in the British Medical Journal actually called for the medical profession to do less screening of patients and to cut back on prescribing treatment – 'to help combat climate change'. Doctors called for global warming concerns to be put above patients' interests.

'The climate emergency is the true health crisis of our time,' was the message from the medical establishment.

Attempts to appease the ever-soaring demands of the insane climate change cultists must, apparently, be made without regard for the safety or comfort of people who are ill. So, to give one small but important example, the doctors who have been suckered in by the climate fraud want traditional inhalers, as used by patients with asthma and other respiratory disorders, to be replaced with dry powder inhalers – ignoring the fact that these are likely to increase the risk of patient dependence and cost more. And also, more importantly, ignoring the fact that there are serious problems with dose uniformity when dry powder inhalers are used. I have no doubt that patients who have grown accustomed to more widely used inhalers will find the dry powder replacements extremely difficult to use. No one among the cultists seems to give a damn about this.

NHS England, which ought to be worrying about improving an appalling service to patients, has spent heaven knows how much producing a report (classification: 'official' – whatever that means) headed 'Delivering a Net Zero National Health Service'.

In 2020, the NHS commissioned an expert panel, chaired by someone called Dr Nick Watts, to set out a 'path' to a 'net zero NHS'. (Watts is an Australian who is Executive Director of the Lancet Countdown: Tracking Progress on Health and Climate Change, regularly consults with the World Health Organisation where he supports the WHOs engagement with the UN Framework Convention on Climate Change.) The utterly absurd strategy is to reach net zero by 2040 for the emissions the NHS controls directly and net zero by 2045 for the emissions the NHS has the ability to influence. Inevitably, one of the recommendations (found on page 67-68 of the report)is 'avoiding staff travel by using video conferencing and increased working from home reduced patient travel through digital GP and outpatient appointments or care provided in the patient's home'. (The shortage of punctuation presumably helps combat global warming in some way.) So, this explains the enthusiasm of GPs for attempting to diagnose and treat patients by telephone or computer – instead of seeing them face to face. I assume that the care provided in the patient's home will be provided by robots or untrained care workers since GPs are now themselves committed to working from home, or their golf club bar, and have declared that seeing sick patients in their homes is a waste of their valuable time and that the transport to and from a patient's home will also damage the environment. (One can assume that transporting untrained care workers to a patient's home does less damage to the climate than transporting a GP would do. This may be because the untrained care worker will travel in a small Ford whereas the GP will travel in a large Mercedes.).

The British Medical Association, the doctors' trade union, has been very active in promoting the frauds. In March 2021, the British Medical Association called for a near elimination of covid-19 from the UK before easing of the lockdown restrictions. (Even though the lockdowns were clearly entirely pointless and destined to kill more people than the rebranded flu.) We must constantly remember that the BMA has through its journals received huge sums of money from the drug industry.

It is no exaggeration to say that the drug industry owns and controls the medical profession. It is, however, driven by what I hope are entirely different motives. The drug companies never want to cure people. Their ideal patient is chronically ill and never dies. The drug industry just wants to make products which people need to take for life. The covid-19 jabs killed many people but also caused a massive amount of long-term damage which is now being treated with very expensive drugs. The people who work for the drug industry are, in my view, among the most despicable criminals on earth, and during and after the fake pandemic I was sickened to see them being praised, applauded and given honours.

The BMA has never had patients' interests at heart and I was not joking when, many years ago, I described the BMA as the patients' enemy. Even though the science shows that mask wearing is useless and dangerous, the BMA chairman called for masks to be mandatory outdoors as well as indoors if there were a risk of coming within six feet six inches of other people.

We should remember that the BMA's members and spokesmen have, over the years, made some terrible mistakes. I am reminded of the AIDS scare. TV and newspapers were united in ignoring the facts and promoting the fear, and I remember repeatedly arguing with BMA representatives on television. They were busily warning us that everyone would be affected by AIDS by the year 2000. I got into trouble for arguing, quite accurately, that the fear had been exaggerated by lobbyists with their own agenda – an agenda which was clearly a forerunner of the covid fraud.

70.

So, if testing and treating patients are to be cut back, as the medical establishment recommends, what are they planning as a replacement?

They're planning an entirely new form of health care in which the patient takes on responsibility for testing and investigating their own symptoms and signs and, in many cases, takes on responsibility for treating themselves at home.

The wretched, unreliable, entirely misleading PCR test enabled bureaucrats and politicians to close hospitals, schools and travel facilities. It was always dangerous (I found and published evidence that people had died because of the PCR test) and it never did what it was supposed to do. But it, and other similarly useless tests, made huge sums of money and became multi-billion-dollar earners for companies in the diagnostics industry. Inevitably, however, the test has been regarded as a valuable Trojan horse. A chief executive from one company making diagnostic tests told the annual JP Morgan Health Care Conference in January 2023 that the test had brought about a wider acceptance of a rapid point-of-care (POC) model. And it is clear that under this paradigm, more diagnostic tests will in future be conducted at or near to the patient's location.

The conspirators' rationale behind this new development is, of course, that if patients can be tested at home, at a supermarket, or at their work, then they don't have to use up precious fuel travelling to the hospital or a doctor's clinic. In the US, Walmart stores are equipped with 'patient service centres where tests can be done and passed directly on for analysis – with the results available to read online or on a smart phone app. Even after a rogue diagnostic company called Theranos was exposed as a fraud, diagnostic start-ups in America raised $5.4 billion in 2020.

Roche, infamous to millions for its promotion of benzodiazepine tranquillisers, makes a handheld device that can detect heart failure with a small blood sample. In the old days a doctor could do this in moments. Today, doctors are too busy organising and supervising vaccination programmes to do anything as practical as listen to a patient's chest or look at their ankles. Tests will soon be available for cancer. And if tests are too complex to perform or be read by the average patient, specially trained health care professionals (with half a day's training in how to perform a specific test) will be deployed – as they were during the mass PCR testing programme around the world.

It's always crucial to remember that the fundamental aim of the conspirators is to save oil by cutting down the amount of travel that 'ordinary' people do (leaving plenty of oil for their yachts, jets and tanks). The home testing paradigm (relying as it does on ineffective tests which will undoubtedly be misread by people who have no medical training) has the added advantage of helping to kill off huge swathes of the population.

Today, there is no doubt that the medical profession is complicit in the Government's attack on the people it is paid to serve.

71.

And finally, of course, the trade unions put the boot in.

I find it utterly impossible not to believe that the unions (including the British Medical Association and the Royal College of Nursing) are part of the plan to destroy health care in the UK, although I suspect that the vast majority of striking staff members – tempted by the prospect of a massive pay rise – are quite unaware of the hidden agenda they are supporting.

In early 2023, it was clear that there was little or no effective health care in the United Kingdom. Dr Adrian Boyle, head of the Royal College of Emergency Medicine, said at the start of the year that 300-500 people a week were dying because of emergency health delays. These delays were, at least in part, undoubtedly caused by the coordinated strikes and it was difficult to understand why the strike leaders had not been charged with murder since their deliberate actions were responsible for many deaths. Normally if an individual does something which kills people, he or she can expect to find themselves in court. Why should union leaders be exempt from normal laws? Most strikers seem to be demanding that they be given pay rises which will match inflation. This sort of mental attitude probably means that most strikers (however menial their task) want to be receiving above the average wage.

72.

During 2022, an astonishing and horrifying 30% of adults in the UK tried, and failed, to obtain an appointment with their GP. Half those frustrated patients then treated themselves or asked a friend to treat them. A number chose to go privately and there is no doubt that consultants who work part time in the National Health Service have made a fortune by seeing patients who could not be seen through the NHS. And, of course, GPs earning £150,000 a year from the NHS for a stunted service have been making huge sums by providing scarcely adequate private services online to other doctors' patients.

All of this has, of course, had a severely damaging effect on the world's economies.

In the UK, for example, the deliberate destruction of the NHS (with long delays for tests and investigations and for treatment) has led to there being millions of working age people who are too sick to work. Similar things have happened around the world.

The international creation of 'long covid' (now a dangerous default diagnosis for any signs of symptoms which occur after a positive PCR test) as a convenient excuse for permanent unemployment, has kept millions out of work and has the added advantage of providing a long-term excuse for permanent unemployment. Post vital fatigue has been known for decades but long covid is something very different and appears to have been created with very specific reasons. The scientific evidence suggests that the vast majority of those claiming to suffer from it are hypochondriacs or are merely avoiding work.

Hospital staff claim that they can do little or nothing about ever lengthening waiting lists because of the number of beds which are blocked by elderly patients who cannot be sent home. This is disingenuous nonsense. If beds are blocked it is because hospital staff have deliberately kept patients in hospital in order to create problems.

The elderly have always been at risk of falling or contracting other health problems, and to insist that an elderly patient must stay in a hospital bed because if they are allowed to go home they may fall over and hurt themselves, is nonsense designed to create problems and satisfy political aims to destroy health care.

I fear that the NHS in the UK (and health care services around the world) had to be destroyed in order to create fear and a sense of loneliness and exclusion from society. And, of course, damaging health care will, by dramatically increasing the number of people unable to work, do great damage to the global economy.

Once you can see the bigger picture it becomes patently clear that everything fits together.

73.

The policy of the conspirators has long been that the elderly should be allowed to die. The United Nations policy (an exercise in officially approved ageism which turned the over 70s into non-citizens) and the Liverpool Care Pathway (a technical term for murder) make it very easy for governments to kill their elderly citizens. In the UK, doctors and nurses are pretty well allowed to do what they like with those who are over 70 years of age – with or without their permission or their relatives' approval. In care homes, even untrained staff can stuff the unknowing, trusting elderly full of benzodiazepines and other toxic substances. (The cut off age for caring will, of course, be reduced over the coming years.) The elderly and their relatives used to have to watch out for DNR (Do Not Resuscitate) notices being stuck on a patient's medical records. That was simple. These days anyone over 70 who goes into hospital is, it seems, a suitable target for the midazolam and morphine 'kill' cocktail which is now in standard use. Every older citizen has constantly to watch their step. One slip or trip could take them into a hospital from which the only exit will be on a shrouded trolley on their way to the undertaker.

'We have to avoid bed blocking patients' is the excuse from members of staff who regard the elderly as subhuman; members of another species who are not entitled to medical care.

In early 2023, Dr Ezekiel Emanuel, the 65-year-old White House oncologist and Obamacare architect, stated that he will refuse all medication (including antibiotics and painkillers) when he turns 75 years of age. His personal cut off point is a decade away so this gives him plenty of time to change his mind or for everyone to forget what he said.

Emanuel is reported to have stated that old age is a burden to society and to loved ones. He claims (erroneously perpetuating a drug company supported myth) that people have more years of life now than before (it is only an improvement in infant mortality figures which has changed and there are more elderly people alive because there are more people alive).He is also reported to have said that old age robs us of creativity and our ability to contribute to work, society and the world. And he adds that the degradation of health means that the elderly can rob a family of valuable time and resources.

It seems clear to me that Dr Emanuel is spouting the sort of nonsense espoused by the conspirators who want to get rid of old people. (And, of course, it is very easy to make those promises now. It will be considerably harder for him to stick to them if and when he reaches his 75th birthday.)

A few years ago I wrote an entire book (called *Climbing Trees at 112*) which lists the many astonishing achievements of elderly individuals (up to the age of 112). Dr Emanuel should read it.

74.

Health services around the world are now devoted to vaccination programmes. Neither doctors nor nurses seem to give a damn about evidence or their ethical responsibilities to their patients.

The evidence proving that the covid-19 jab is useless and unsafe is overwhelming. Even governments now admit that the jab won't prevent you getting covid-19 or spreading it if you do get it. And the figures for the disease itself have been distorted and fiddled. I've proved conclusively that covid-19, the re-branded flu, has not killed more people than the ordinary flu. Not surprisingly, no one will debate the figures with me because the official statistics prove my point emphatically.

I know that establishment figures will never debate – because all the facts are on my side and they will lose – but we have to tell people, and keep telling people, that the authorities refuse to debate because their refusal proves that they are lying and deceiving and that they know they are lying and deceiving.

75.

It has been proved beyond question that the short-term risks for those accepting the covid-19 jabs are horrific – worse than the risks associated with any traditional, mass market vaccine that's ever been made.

It was known in late 2020, two years ago, that the covid-19 jabs would cause heart trouble, strokes, neurological problems, myocarditis and pericarditis. My 300 plus videos have been removed from YouTube and were for months removed from BrandNewTube but most of them – the ones we could find – are now on www.vernoncoleman.org. And all the transcripts – even for the missing videos – are also on the site. So you can check everything I've said since February 2020. Transcripts are also available in two books *Covid-19: The Greatest Fraud in History* and *Covid-19: Exposing Lies*.

The jab induced deaths we're already seeing are going to get worse and include heart attacks, myocarditis, blood clots and, of course, massive immune system problems.

How many of those who were jabbed will die of colds, flu and so on?

The authorities will claim the deaths are caused by new and more virulent infections. They'll ignore the evidence. The death rate is rising, partly because of the lockdowns and partly because there is no effective health care now in many countries – particularly the UK – but most of the sudden deaths will be caused by the covid-19 jabs.

I believe the vaxxed will be extremely vulnerable to new variations of the flu. They will constantly be encouraged to accept new jabs, new booster jabs and so on. The ignorant, the fearful and the susceptible will become pincushions, the drug companies will make untold billions in profits and the medical profession will be paid huge fees to give the jabs.

76.

More and more women who have been jabbed and do get pregnant will have miscarriages or give birth to under-developed babies. Or the babies will have serious heart problems. Many babies will doubtless be lost mid-term or born dead. Medical history is littered with examples of drugs which everyone said were safe but which turned out to be not so safe. Thalidomide is just one of many drugs in that history.

And what will happen when those babies grow up? Will they be completely infertile? What other problems will they develop? The mRNA jab is an entirely new type of product. No one can tell you exactly what is going to happen. No one can tell you what will happen in five, ten or fifteen years. We have to wait and see. And before anyone sneers, let me remind you that there have been drugs which have affected the children of women who took them.

The drug diethylstilboestrol (DES) is a manufactured version of oestrogen. It was given to pregnant women to prevent miscarriages. It was thought to be safe though it was useless for this. In 1971, it was found that the drug caused cancer and doctors in America stopped prescribing it. Doctors in Europe carried on for another seven years.

But there's a twist. It later became clear that the daughters of women who took DES while they were pregnant were at increased risk of developing several types of cancer. I wrote about this in my book *Paper Doctors* in 1977 – and European doctors then stopped prescribing it for pregnant women. It took 40 years for the cancers to become apparent.

The cancer risk for the vaxxed cannot be under-estimated. No one knows what will happen.

There are already early signs of problems with doctors reporting an increase in cancers among patients who have been jabbed. Some of the cancers are new and some are cancers which have come back after being dormant for some time.

Will the vaxxed be a threat to those around them? Well, yes, I fear they will. They will carry some infections without showing symptoms or signs and so I suspect they'll spread those infections. I reported a long time ago on the theory that immunosuppressed individuals could provide a reservoir in which viruses might more easily mutate.

And will the vaxxed be vulnerable if they mix with the unvaxxed? Well, again, yes I fear they will. The immune systems of the vaxxed have been changed forever. Just how vulnerable they will be is a big mystery.

The problem is that the authorities will not be honest about any of this. They claim that covid-19 deaths among the vaxxed are caused by new variations and whenever they can they will, of course, blame the wise ones who have refused to allow themselves to be jabbed with the most deadly, toxic brew ever invented and promoted to billions by governments, drug companies and the medical establishment.

And, of course, they blame all the side effects of the vaccine on a fake designer disease which they call 'long covid' and which they are using to help destroy economies. (The ordinary, old-fashioned flu can cause post viral fatigue but this was never previously regarded as a major concern.)

And will the jabs have any effect on the brains of the vaxxed? Well, I'd be surprised if they didn't. Anything which seems to affect circulatory system and the immune system seems likely to affect the brain in some way. Apart from major bleeds what is going to happen to the intelligence of the jabbed? I've dealt with this hazard at some length and the evidence is on my websites.

All the rules about testing and trialling new drugs have been ignored. Everything has been rushed – for absolutely no good reason.

In one of my videos I counted ten ways in which the giving of the covid-19 jab is unscientific. Those doctors who are involved in this massive, uncontrolled, global experiment should be struck off the medical register and put in jail for life. Instead they are being rewarded with huge amounts of money and much praise.

No mainstream journalists dare to question what is being done – even though there is clearly very little science to this experiment and what little science exists is being ignored. Their cowardice is unprecedented.

Despite all this, and despite the clear evidence that the mRNA covid-19 jabs didn't do what they were supposed to do, and are causing a global torrent of death and injury (largely blamed on anything and everything else), drug companies are now busy manufacturing a whole range of new mRNA products – including a variety of new vaccines and drugs for the treatment of cancer.

The failure of the covid-19 jabs does not seem to have slowed down the medical establishment's enthusiasm for these untested products which will, I fear, soon be offered widely to billions of gullible and trusting people.

Meanwhile, those of us who question this fraud and who question the complete lack of science behind what is happening, are demonised and attacked.

The savage, cruel silencing and demonization of the medical truth-tellers is all the evidence we need that the alleged covid-19 pandemic is the greatest fraud in history. It has been inspired, maintained and promoted, without mercy, by the most evil people the world has ever seen. And the medical establishment must now include itself as part of the conspiracy of evil threatening our present and our future.

Parents who allow their children to be used in this experiment should be charged with child abuse. Politicians and journalists who blindly promote mass vaccination programmes are ignorant, bigoted and dangerous.

We need a moratorium on vaccination which is, I believe, doing infinitely more harm than good.

But I'll settle for a national, live debate on the subject.

They won't dare do that, of course. I know that.

They won't dare, because they'll lose the debate. Instead of debating, the cowards and the liars will just continue to lie and spread abuse.

And that should tell you everything you need to know.

77.

It's all about money. Drug companies are making billions out of vaccines. Doctors are making millions out of giving vaccinations.

The climate change industry is a commercial scam – just like AIDS – and there are huge numbers of people making big money out of it.

The billions being demanded in reparation payments will be siphoned off by climate change crooks and pressure groups

78.

Here's a little piece of irony.

In January 2023, Michele Donelan, the UK's culture secretary defended the right of Jeremy Clarkson to write a column expressing his views about Meghan Markle. Clarkson had caused a furore by saying that he had dreamt of her being paraded naked through the streets and having lumps of excrement thrown at her.

The culture secretary said: 'I believe in freedom of speech very strongly…I think he had the right to say what he wanted to say.'

How strange then that in the same week a Tory MP had the whip removed by her Government for daring to express his views about the danger of the covid-19 jabs.

And how strange that I have been banned by all mainstream media, YouTube, most publishers and all social media for telling the truth.

79.

In early 2022, the west engineered a war between Russia and Ukraine by using NATO to threaten the Russian premier.

The designer war was immediately taken up by the media and by western politicians who suddenly introduced financial sanctions which seemed deliberately designed to push Russia into introducing its own sanctions which would, inevitably, push up fuel and food prices in the West.

The odd thing about this designer war is not only that Russia had invaded Ukraine before, without anyone in the West seeming to notice or to care, but that other wars taking place in Syria and Yemen were just as violent and just as unreasonable but were pretty well ignored by Western politicians, media and campaigners. Town Halls all over the UK were flying the Ukraine flag, as mainstream journalists encourage everyone to think only about the war in Ukraine.

Looking at the news you'd have thought that Ukraine was the only trouble spot in the world.

But you'd have been wrong.

At the time that the world's people were encouraged to concentrate their thoughts on Ukraine, the number of civilian deaths in Ukraine was (according to the United Nations) 760. According to the Ukraine President, the number of soldiers who have died in Ukraine is 1,300.

However, according to the United Nations, the seven-year-old war in Yemen had killed an estimated 377,000 people by the end of 2021 – and was killing far more people than the fighting in Ukraine.

The Yemen war has been described as the largest humanitarian crisis in the world.

The war in Syria had been going on for ten years and the number of people killed was believed to be 610,000

As far as I know no town halls were flying flags in support of the people of Yemen and Syria. There was virtually no media coverage of these wars.

It was clear that the invasion of Ukraine was organised and manipulated by the conspirators in the West to help create the energy and food shortages required for the Great Reset and the New World Order that they had planned for us.

Other wars had also been ignored. For example, how many of those waving Ukraine flags have even heard of the Moldo-Russian Transnistrian war in which Transnistria fought for independence from Moldova. Most Western journalists have probably never even heard of Transnistria even though private homes were attacked and civilians were targeted.

80.

As the economic news around the world got steadily worse, the press around the world helped cover up essential truths by giving an enormous amount of publicity to the rather unseemly, undignified whinging of a multimillionaire, who is approaching middle age and who has an exaggerated sense of personal worth and an almost painful sense of entitlement. Having released a ghost written autobiography which seemed to be little more than a standard kiss and tell tale, revealing private thoughts and incidents, king Charles's second son, Harry seemed pathetically desperate for fame and money at any cost.

But the book was used as a distraction.

As Harry sold his soul for a large mess of potage and excoriated his family, the media lapped up the childish revelations and took full advantage of the opportunity to suppress and smother the startling truths about the damage being done by the experimental jabs, and the awful future faced by Britons deprived of a health service and facing a steady, long-term slide into a painful economic depression.

81.

There are people around the world who think that the Chinese firm approach to covid-19 was the correct one, and who admire the social credit system which is now very much a part of life in China. These are usually the same people who believe that in 2020 the world was devastated by a pandemic and who also believe that we are all threatened by man-made climate change.

It is worth remembering that in order to try to reach its zero-covid target, China forcibly sealed citizens in their apartment blocks, sent citizens to mandatory isolation centres and made people take a test before allowing them to enter a supermarket.

I believe that the absurd rules about covid which have been introduced in China are all part of their compliance training programme – an essential part of the social credit system. (I have described social credit in detail in my book *Social Credit: Nightmare on your Street*).

Countries in the west have followed the social credit system (which was created in China) because it fits very well into the programme for the Great Reset.

Incidentally, I do not believe that China is committed to the Great Reset or the idea of a world government which is an essential feature of the New Normal.

Some years ago, China instituted a rule forbidding couples to have more than one child. This was however replaced by a law allowing couples to have two children. The Chinese are now encouraging couples to have three children. This goes against the conspirators' determination to cut the world population from eight billion to five hundred million. I suspect that the Chinese have relaxed the rules about children because they don't want to fall into the problem affecting Japan and many Western countries whereby falling birth-rates mean that there will soon not be enough young people to pay tax and look after the elderly.

I also suspect that the Chinese like the idea of growing their population at the same time as other countries reduce their populations. It fits in with their desire to take over the world but to do it slowly; day by day, month by month, year by year and decade by decade. The Chinese, remember, have always taken a long view.

In 1972, China's Zhou Enlai was asked what he thought of the French Revolution. He is allegedly to have replied that it was too early to say.

82.

Chatbots ,whereby a real person talks, via a computer or smart phone, to someone who appears to be a real person but who is in reality merely a computer programme, are becoming increasingly common. Students are even using them to write their essays for them.

The problem, of course, is that chatbots merely regurgitate the nonsense with which they are programmed.

And it is quite inevitable that they will prove to be as biased and as one sided as Google or YouTube. No chatbot is every going to provide a balanced view of a so-called pandemic or of climate change, for example.

83.

I wrote the following 35 years ago in a book called *The Health Scandal*.

'By the year 2020, one third of the population in the developed world will be over the age of sixty five. One quarter of the population will be diabetic. In every home where there are two healthy parents and two healthy children, there will be four disabled or dependent individuals needing constant care. Diseases such as blindness (which is ten times as common among the over 65s and thirty times as common among the over 75s) will be as common as indigestion and hay-fever are today. Unemployment will be normal. Stress related diseases will be endemic. Developed countries around the world will face bankruptcy as they struggle to find the cash to pay pensions, sick pay and unemployment benefits.

Resentment, bitterness and anger will divide the young and the old, the able-bodied and the dependent, the employed and the unemployed. There will be anarchy despair and civil war. There will be ghettoes of elderly and disabled citizens abandoned to care for themselves. There will be armed guards on our hospitals. Those with jobs will travel to work in armoured cars.

For years those who have forecast the end of the human race have talked of nuclear war, starvation in the Third World and pollution as being the major threats to our survival. But the decline I predict for the year 2020 will be triggered not by any of these forces but by much simpler and entirely predictable developments. The human race will be destroyed by medical ambition, commercial greed and political opportunism.'

From The Health Scandal by Vernon Coleman, published 1988

84.

In January 2023, the UK Government (which already had the greatest debts in history and the highest taxes since the Second World War) announced that people receiving benefits (paid for by taxpayers) could continue to claim their benefits if they got jobs.

85.

Anyone objecting to anything the conspirators do is denounced as a Far Right Activist. Always.

86.

Health care services of all varieties are going to continue to deteriorate.

Genuinely bed-bound elderly people obviously need a hospital or nursing home but many old people find themselves living in appalling conditions in care homes without considering the alternatives.

I have for many years argued that many old people would be far more comfortable (and likely to be treated with more kindness, respect and dignity) if they lived in a hotel rather than a care home. Hotel accommodation would in most cases be considerably cheaper and, while providing meals, laundry services and freedom from worry about utility bills, it would also provide far more independence. Patients in care homes are often prevented from seeing relatives, or from leaving the home in which they are effectively incarcerated. But no hotel is going to tell its guests that they cannot see relatives or friends. Hotel accommodation can provide excellent assisted living – a halfway house between complete independence and complete dependence.

An alternative favoured by many people these days is life on board a cruise ship. Some take a cruise for two or three months and then swap to another ship when that cruise is completed. Personal belongings which are too cumbersome to be carried around but too valuable (in whatever terms) to be abandoned or sold can be put into storage. Short spells between cruises can be spent in a hotel. Modern cruise ships are equipped with doctors, hospitals, libraries and numerous opportunities for games and meeting people. The food is likely to be infinitely better than the food provided in care homes. Life on a cruise shop isn't for everyone but many find it an excellent way to live. They can be alone in their cabin or a quiet corner of the ship when they want to be and they can be entertained and meet new people when the fancy takes them. Life on board a cruise ship is unlikely to be as expensive as life in a care home.

87.

At the start of 2022, the global stock market was worth $110 trillion and the global bond market was worth $130 trillion.

During 2022, the world's investors lost $100 trillion worldwide in shares, bonds, businesses and property. Anyone who has a pension fund will have been involved in this massive, unprecedented loss. Stock markets lost nearly 20% (with technology stocks losing 32.5%) and bonds lost 16%. Investors who had shares in Russian companies were effectively wiped out and saw their holdings reduced to nil.

All these holdings had been driven up by artificially lowered interest rates. As soon as interest rates started to rise, the collapse began and countless millions of people around the world suddenly woke up and found they were not as well-off as they thought they were. Millions of people with pension funds probably won't realise how much money they've lost (or has been lost on their behalf) until they receive their next pension statement. Millions who were relying on their investments to pay off their mortgages will find themselves without the money to pay off the mortgage and with a property which is worth far less than they paid for it. Many may then remember the infamous line 'you will own nothing and be happy', credited to the World Economic Forum. And, although they may accept that they own nothing (or next to nothing) they may wonder about the 'be happy' bit of the quote. Millennials and generation Z investors will be particularly 'lost' since they have no experience of high inflation or higher interest rates. Many will have put much or all of their money into crypto-currencies and will suffer huge losses.

When interest rates rose, everything else collapsed. But governments and banks are displaying their intentions by putting up interest rates for borrowers while keeping them pitifully low for savers, far lower than inflation – ensuring that savers cannot make any money and are, indeed losing money every day, every month and every year, and will be pushed into spending (thereby becoming poor and losing their financial independence).

I believe that the stock markets are doomed for at least a decade and probably forever. We are heading for a permanent recession (which will soon be redefined as a financial depression). Many people will probably think that this does not affect them – but it does. Anyone who has a job, or who has savings, or who has, or hopes to have a pension, or who receives money from their government will be affected. (And that means everyone – including civil servants).

These are dangerous times to have debts (and by that I include property loans such as mortgages) unless you have a long-term fixed rate loan which you are happy you can manage without difficulty. I would be very worried about taking on a floating rate loan. And, incidentally, I suspect that renting property could soon be a real problem (there is, of course, already a scarcity of homes to rent) as a constant stream of new legislation and taxes make life for landlords increasingly difficult and unprofitable. This seems to be a special problem in the UK and many landlords (particularly those who have just one or two properties) will be selling what they have.

I think that everyone with savings (and a pension fund which isn't provided by taxpayers counts as savings) should, whenever possible, plan and control their own investments. I fear (as I have done for some years now) that many of those who work for the Government and expect to receive the generous, inflation-proofed government pension which they have been promised, will be very disappointed. Future governments will not be able to fulfil the promises made by previous governments.

Rules and regulations which govern these things ensure that I am not allowed to tell you how to invest but I can tell you how I've been investing for some years now and how I plan to continue to invest in the future. What you choose to do is, of course, up to you.

I will look to hold value shares (which have solid, preferably global businesses which provide essential goods or services) and I will give preference to companies which have few or no debts and which pay decent dividends.

I will avoid growth companies which promise profits in the future but which are currently dependent upon loans from banks and which are likely to need more cash in the future –either from banks or from shareholders.

I will buy shares in gold and oil and mining companies, especially those which dig out metals used in the manufacture of electric cars and so on. I will buy shares in companies which dig up coal (because I suspect it will continue to be used) and those which find uranium (because more and more countries are going to turn to nuclear power). I am not in the slightest bit interested in satisfying the demands of ESG enthusiasts (who have consistently lied and exaggerated and who cannot be trusted) but I am extremely interested in looking after my family.

Generally speaking, I will not buy shares in companies which cater exclusively to the British because Britain is 'stuffed'. (In 2012 I wrote a book called *Stuffed!* which was subtitled *Why there is now no hope for England and the English; why we are doomed to generations of penury, depression and social strife; who is to blame and why the only solution to our nation's woes is a revolution*.)

British retail companies and British companies selling services (in hotels and cafes for example) seem to me to have a very bleak future. I do not believe that the Great British Pound is a healthy currency for investment purposes. I say this even though share prices in Britain have been kept artificially low as the world (controlled by conspirators who regard the European Union as the blueprint for their world government) blames Brexit for all our ills.

Although I can't see property as much of an investment in the UK (until prices have fallen by at least a quarter) I suspect that this might be a good time to buy real assets which are likely to hold their value. Antique furniture and jewellery such as watches can sometimes be bought at auction remarkably cheaply. (You don't have to attend an auction to buy, of course. Online auctions can sometimes be remarkably good places to buy good items as long as you know what you want to buy, know the rules of the site you are using, know something about the items you're considering to purchase and do your research very thoroughly.) Keeping cash in the bank is certain to lose you money because I suspect that inflation is going to stay far higher than interest rates for some considerable time.

I will buy shares in storage companies which provide warehouse space for internet giants and packaging companies which make the cardboard boxes which internet companies use. These, I feel, are like investing in spades and pickaxes during the Californian gold rush.

88.

The fake pandemic and the ubiquitous jabbing with a toxic jab that didn't do what they said it would do, and wasn't as safe as they promised it would be, was all just a training programme.

Like the utterly pointless recycling programme (diesel lorries collecting recycling and diesel powered ships taking it abroad to be dumped or burnt in China or Turkey) it was all an exercise in compliance.

The feeble-minded and weak-willed wore their masks, hid indoors and allowed themselves to be jabbed. They preferred to believe drug company lies rather than listen to the truth and now they are dying in their thousands. Those who trusted the establishment are doomed. They made their choice. But they made the wrong choice.

The elderly, the young, the sick, the disabled, the self-employed, those running small businesses have all been punished for living. The evil conspirators have no compassion, no empathy, no sense of community. They have paid brainwashing specialists to create fear and they've forced upon millions a toxic jab that causes brain and heart damage.

The beginning of the saga isn't difficult to find.

It all started when peak oil was first recognised in the 1940s. The conspirators, or their fathers and grandfathers, realised that they needed to protect the oil supplies by cutting travel and changing our way of living. They also decided they needed to cut the size of the global population. (Incidentally, as anyone who has studied the facts will know the nonsensical rumour that oil is not a fossil fuel and not running out was created by the conspirators and their misinformation specialists to cause confusion and help them cover up the truth. I put this piece of nonsense in the same category as the ludicrous notion that the earth is flat, and that if we travel too far we'll fall off the edge.)

In the 1960s, the first generation of modern conspirators deliberately dug the decades old myth of man-made global warming out of the history books, dusted it off and re-launched it as a man-made scare story designed to terrify and control the gullible and the feeble-minded. It's done very nicely for them but it's about as scientific as the theory that the earth is flat. The United Nations was there early on. The World Economic Forum came in later. There was never a shred of evidence for any of it. The only thing man-made about our weather has been the carefully planned and orchestrated series of events designed to shock and kill and reduce a global population which they think is too large. It is no coincidence that the worst cold spell in recent British history coincides with the highest fuel prices in history. And then, when they decided we'd had enough cold weather, they allowed the temperature to rise in a sudden, unprecedented way. Most people still don't realise just how much the conspirators are manipulating our weather, though one would have thought everyone would have noticed just how easy it seems to be for the authorities to make sure that there is good weather for ceremonial occasions, royal weddings and big sporting events.

(And here's another oddity. The WHO has traditionally said that indoor temperatures should be kept at 70 degrees F for the elderly. But the mainstream media says that 60 will do fine. And, of course, covid regulations mean the windows must be kept open so that the freezing cold air can come inside and do its worst. The result will be that 100,000 elderly folk will die of the cold each winter – murdered by a combination of circumstances.)

And then, impressed by what the Chinese were doing, western governments co-opted social credit schemes, added them to digitalisation and started to promise us the Great Reset – a new world order, a new way of living where we would do what we were told and live in a world of permanent fear: the world Orwell foresaw when he wrote *1984*.

The designer war with Russia and the completely unnecessary sanctions were dreamt up and introduced to push up energy prices and create food shortages. Britain alone has spent tens of billions on providing arms for a war between the West and Russia – even though our participation in that war has never been officially declared. The real aim was to kill hundreds of millions in Africa and Asia where small rises in fuel and food costs cause a massive rise in starvation. The conspirators knew that if they distracted voters in the West no one would notice the cleansing and genocide taking place in another part of the world – and they were right.

Governments have encouraged the removal of statues, micro-aggression, allegations of racism and sexism built out of nothing and the blocking of roads by lunatic climate cultists. The entire climate change fraud can be summed up in one word: hypocrisy. Every year 45,000 insane cultists fly around the world to another conference where they agree that no one should fly anywhere. Many of them arrive by private plane.

The endless hypocrisy is utterly staggering. Canadian Mark Carney, probably the worst ever Governor of the Bank of England, turned himself into a climate expert and loves telling us all what to do to save the planet from the perils of pseudoscience. But he's been selling farms in Brazil which are linked to deforestation claims.

Most independent scientists agree that the idea of man-made climate change is manufactured nonsense and that even if the absurd predictions shared by ignorant fools come true, the effect will be of no consequence. The real problems in our world are man-made it is true, but they have nothing to do with the climate.

Royals and celebrities who tell us we must not fly or have big families, fly by private plane and have big families. The climate fraud, like the AIDS fraud, is a pseudoscientific marketing exercise and it's all about money.

Back in the 1990s, we were told that AIDS would affect us all by the turn of the century. To try to keep it going, the authorities now label thousands who have tuberculosis as AIDS sufferers. The AIDS fraud was a trial run for covid but it failed – as did various other attempts.

Today, lunatic schemes mean that it is nigh on impossible for anyone who isn't rich to drive into London. In Oxford they're planning to effectively imprison citizens in the name of climate change.

Global warming is now blamed for everything bad that happens. But in truth, everything bad that happens has been deliberately arranged. The inflation which is devastating every country was foreseeable and inevitable. If you doubt me take a look at my recent video entitled 'I warned about soaring inflation and interest rates in 2020, so what's next'. The video is on www.vernoncoleman.org and the transcript is there too. If I knew what was coming over two years ago, do you not think the central banks might have worked it out?

I believe they coordinated the mass of strikes that have devastated everything so that they could further decimate economies which were already crumbling. The self-employed will suffer most from the strikes and most will go out of business – deliberately destroyed by governments and unions working together. When school teachers go on strike (or refuse to work for an entirely spurious reason such as fear of catching the flu) parents in the UK have a legal right to take time off work. (That is a great help for the nation's productivity figures.)

Economies everywhere are being devastated by insane four day working weeks and insane working from home policies. Postal services are being devastated by strikes which will force everyone to do everything online. By the middle of December 2022, the rail strikes had lost the country an estimated £2-3 billion even though subsidising the railways has cost British households £1,800 each over the past six years.

The feeble-minded think the unions are hoping to bring down the Government by their actions. Nothing could be further from the truth. We already have a communist government controlled by the WEF. I believe the unions are destroying the economy and the country and collaborating in a race to drive us into inflation hell and a world in which we will own nothing and be as miserable as sin. Pay rises at or above inflation levels will simply push inflation ever higher and create poverty and destroy currencies.

And still there are people around who think it's all happening by accident, that we're having a lot of bad luck and that one coincidence after another just keeps on coming. The mainstream media is full of woefully ignorant commentators moaning that the world has gone inexplicably mad. But the people in control are insane. But their madness is defined and very carefully controlled. Schwab doesn't think he's a teapot. Bill Gates doesn't think he is Napoleon and His Royal Hypocrite doesn't think he's a banana. They all know exactly what they're doing. And populations everywhere have allowed them to get away with murder.

Nothing is now happening by accident. There are no coincidences. Everything bad that is happening is part of a master-plan and once you know that, it's easy to see what comes next. You and I may be described as conspiracy theorists but they are conspiracy practitioners.

Every time something bad happens just ask yourself: 'Who benefits from this – and exactly how will they benefit?'

And ask yourself how the conspirators stand to profit. Remember they are a potent mixture of hypocritical left wingers who are indistinguishable from communists, and a bunch of greedy billionaire tricksters who are nothing more than raw fascists.

And if you think it is strange to suggest that communists would work with fascists, consider this: if politics is a straight line with communists at one end and fascists at the other and you then turn the straight line into a circle, then the communists and the fascists stand side by side because their aims and methods are indistinguishable.

The conspirators and their hand maidens, collaborators , people such as politicians, academics, broadcasters, government advisors, newspaper editors and the medical establishment, will tell you that inflation will soon be under control, that interest rates will go back to nothing, that fuel and food prices will soon be normal again and that all we have to worry about is the climate cultists' hysterical and nonsensical claims that the Eiffel Tower will be entirely under water by a week on Wednesday and that the Statue of Liberty will have melted by the following Tuesday.

89.

The richest people in Britain are leaving. Just where they are going is something of a mystery since there are no safe, secure countries left and all countries are introducing the same lunatic laws at much the same pace. The chances are that if you leave country A and go to country B to escape horrendous new restrictions, the same restrictions will be introduced in country B before you've had time to unpack and find somewhere to live.

It does seem to me, however, that living in a large town or city is the worst choice. In a town or city you are more likely to be at the mercy of town planners and politicians determined to stamp their control on your life and to restrict your movements. In the wilds of the countryside you might find transport difficult if cars are banned or fuel supplies strictly controlled. The best choice is probably a small town or large village somewhere with a home within cycling distance of a railway station and a supermarket. And fewer CCTV cameras than you're likely to find in a town or a city.

Eventually, of course, small towns and villages will be closed and the inhabitants moved out. The buildings will be left, abandoned, eventually growing to look like those drowned villages which emerge when reservoirs dry up in long, hot summers.

We all have to reassess our priorities and to recognise that nothing that is happening is happening by accident. Too much attention is being paid to effect and not enough to cause.

During the months and years which lie ahead there is going to be much more fear and many more lies will be told. The media will attempt to distract the public from the truth with a seemingly unending series of unbelievably tacky stories about the royal family. The fears will be created by brainwashing specialists, psy-op specialists and psychologists specially hired by governments (as happened during the early days of the fake pandemic).

If they cannot make us sufficiently afraid they will take steps to destroy us and if they cannot do that they will simply kill more of us. If you don't believe that then I am afraid that you simply haven't been paying attention.

There will be more and more taxes. I can see global taxes and specific health warnings printed on meat and meat products within two years if not before – in the same way that there are massive taxes and warnings on tobacco.

And the conspirators are attacking vegetarian eating so that they can sell us a diet of wasps, locusts and factory made garbage.

Small businesses and the self-employed are doomed to a long struggle with the inevitable. Pubs, cafes and small, independent shops have no future because there is no place for them in the New Normal. The Great Reset doesn't have a place for independent businesses any more than it has a place for independent thinking. Millennials, who think we are going back to low interest rates and low inflation are living alongside Peter Pan in James Barrie's Never-Never Land. There will be no more cheap imports from China.

We're already well into extra time. If we don't take action very quickly it will soon all be over. As we move remorselessly into a digital, cashless world, the ghettos I warned about nearly three years ago are getting more and more real every day. No one will save us. We have to save ourselves.

We need to stay alert. The latest danger is that they are planning to make it a war crime to tell the truth about vaccines, of all kinds, or about global warming. Telling the truth is going to be branded alongside terrorism as a crime against humanity.

And the real proof, remember, as with vaccination, is that they won't debate climate change. No discussion is allowed. The media, such as the discredited BBC, have banned all discussion and questioning of vaccination. And they've pretty well banned all discussion of global warming. They pretend that these issues are accepted. But they're only accepted by the conspirators.

Remember, the world is awash with masses of evidence proving that vaccines do more harm than good but the establishment continues to deny that such evidence even exists. There is absolutely no doubt that the covid-19 jabs do massively more harm than good. But doctors and nurses keep on giving them – deliberately poisoning their patients and being paid for it. And patients who need blood transfusions and who ask for unvaxed blood are abused by doctors and nurses. Parents who ask for their children to be given unvaxxed blood are likely to have their children taken away from them. We have no freedom and we have no free speech. Things are so bad that many scientists writing research papers are self-censoring because they are terrified of losing their careers. The world has become a place for people who like taking orders from malignant, cryptorchid cretins.

And remember: when you see something bad happening you have to stand up for what you believe to be right. If you don't then you might as well be dead.

And remember this too: Most of the people who don't believe in coincidences are still alive. That is no coincidence.

Postscript

Even if you don't believe me about the causes of what is happening, you will, I think, find it impossible to deny that strange, unprecedented things are happening and that we must, therefore, look for solutions to the visible consequences of what is happening, even if we find the causes difficult to accept.

Biography of the author

Vernon Coleman was an angry young man for as long as it was decently possible. He then turned into an angry middle-aged man. And now, with no effort whatsoever, he has matured into being an angry old man. He is, he confesses, just as angry as he ever was. Indeed, he may be even angrier because, he says, the more he learns about life the more things he finds to be angry about.

Cruelty, prejudice and injustice are the three things most likely to arouse his well-developed sense of ire but he admits that, at a pinch, inefficiency, incompetence and greed will do almost as well.

The author has an innate dislike of taking orders, a pathological contempt for pomposity, hypocrisy and the sort of unthinking political correctness which attracts support from Guardian reading pseudo-intellectuals. He also has a passionate loathing for those in authority who do not understand that unless their authority is tempered with compassion and a sense of responsibility the end result must always be an extremely unpleasant brand of totalitarianism.

Vernon Coleman qualified as a doctor in 1970 and has worked both in hospitals and as a principal in general practice. He has organised many campaigns concerning iatrogenesis, drug addiction and the abuse of animals and has given evidence to committees at the House of Commons and the House of Lords. Dr Coleman's campaigns have often proved successful. For example, after a 15 year campaign (which started in 1973) he eventually persuaded the British Government to introduce stricter controls governing the prescribing of benzodiazepine tranquillisers. 'Dr Vernon Coleman's articles, to which I refer with approval, raised concern about these important matters,' said the Parliamentary Secretary for Health in the House of Commons in 1988.

Coleman has worked as a columnist for numerous national newspapers including The Sun, The Daily Star, The Sunday Express, The Sunday Correspondent and The People. He once wrote three columns at the same time for different national papers (he wrote them under three different names) At the same time he was also writing weekly columns for the Evening Times in Glasgow and for the Sunday Scot. His syndicated columns have appeared in over 50 regional newspapers in the UK and in newspapers and magazines around the world. He has contributed articles and stories to hundreds of other publications including The Sunday Times, Observer, Guardian, Daily Telegraph, Sunday Telegraph, Daily Express, Daily Mail, Mail on Sunday, Daily Mirror, Sunday Mirror, Punch, Woman, Woman's Own, The Lady, Spectator and British Medical Journal. He was the founding editor of the British Clinical Journal.

For many years he wrote a monthly newsletter. He has lectured doctors and nurses on a variety of medical matters. Tens of millions have consulted his telephone advice lines, watched his videos and visited his websites. He has lectured doctors and students at Birmingham University and St Thomas's Medical School and has given professional evidence to committees in both the House of Commons and the House of Lords.

He has presented numerous programmes on television and radio and was the original breakfast television doctor. He was television's first agony uncle (on BBC1's The Afternoon Show) and presented three TV series based on his bestselling book Bodypower. In the now long-gone days when producers and editors were less wary of annoying the establishment he was a regular broadcaster on many radio and television programmes.

After publication of his books 'The Medicine Men and Paper Doctors in the 1970s, Dr Vernon Coleman was acknowledged to be the world's leading authority on prescription drug side effects and on iatrogenesis.

Today he is considered dangerous and is, therefore, banned from all mainstream media and his books are no longer reviewed in newspapers where editors hope to be remembered in the honours lists.

In the 1980s he wrote the algorithms for the first computerised health programmes – which sold in 26 countries to those far-sighted individuals who had bought the world's first home computers.

In the UK his books have been published by Arrow, Pan, Penguin, Corgi, Mandarin, Star, Piatkus, RKP, Thames and Hudson, Sidgwick and Jackson, Macmillan and many other leading publishing houses. English language versions sell around the world as well as the UK. Several of his books have appeared on both the Sunday Times, Daily Mail and Bookseller bestseller lists. His books have now sold over three million copies in the UK, been translated into 26 languages and sell in over 50 countries. His bestselling non-fiction book 'Bodypower' was voted one of the 100 most popular books of the 1980s/90s and was turned into two television series in the UK. His novel Mrs Caldicot's Cabbage War has been filmed and is, like many of his other novels, available in an audio version.

He has written books under at least 18 pen names and has, in addition, written numerous articles under a vast variety of pennames. His work has also been included in many anthologies including the Penguin Book of 21st Century Protest. He has contributed to various encyclopaedias.

Vernon Coleman has worked for the Open University in the UK and was an honorary Professor of Holistic Medical Sciences at the Open International University based in Sri Lanka.

Today, he likes books, films and writing. He writes, reads and collects books and has a larger library than most towns. He has never been much of an athlete, though he once won a certificate for swimming a width of the public baths in Walsall and once swam a mile for charity. He finished after everyone else had gone home and had switched off the lights.

Coleman likes pens and notebooks and used to enjoy watching cricket until the authorities sold out and allowed people to paint slogans on the grass. His interests and hobbies include animals, books, photography, drawing, chess, backgammon, cinema, philately, billiards, sitting in cafés and on benches and collecting Napoleana and old books that were written and published before dust-wrappers were invented. He likes log fires and bonfires, motor racing and music by Beethoven, Mozart and Mahler and dislikes politicians, bureaucrats and cauliflower cheese. He considers himself an expert on bonfires and while some people can taste a wine and tell you they can smell raspberries, potatoes, old socks and wet peat he can sniff a bonfire and tell you what is being burnt.

Vernon Coleman has co-written five books with his wife, Donna Antoinette Coleman who is a talented oil painter whose work has been exhibited. She is the author of My Quirky Cotswold Garden.

Vernon and Antoinette Coleman have been happily married for more than 20 years and they live in the delightful if isolated village of Bilbury in Devon where they have designed for themselves a unique world to sustain and nourish them in these dark and difficult times. He enjoys malt whisky, toasted muffins and old films.

Vernon, who is devoted to Donna Antoinette, the kindest, sweetest, most sensitive woman a man could hope to meet, can ride a bicycle and swim, though not at the same time. Although not terribly musical he decided to learn how to play the harmonica 64 years ago. He now owns three mouth organs, three instruction books, two instruction videos and an instruction audio tape and hopes to find time soon to begin his studies.

Reference Articles referring to Vernon Coleman (Included to counter some of the lies on the internet)
Ref 1
'Volunteer for Kirkby' – The Guardian, 14.5.1965
(Article re VC's work in Kirkby, Liverpool as a Community Service Volunteer in 1964-5)
Ref 2
'Bumbledom forced me to leave the NHS' – Pulse, 28.11.1981
(Vernon Coleman resigns as a GP after refusing to disclose confidential information on sick note forms)
Ref 3
'I'm Addicted To The Star' – The Star, 10.3.1988
Ref 4
'Medicine Becomes Computerised: Plug In Your Doctor.' – The Times, 29.3.1983
Ref 5

'Computer aided decision making in medicine' – British Medical Journal, 8.9.1984 and 27.10.1984
Ref 6
'Conscientious Objectors' – Financial Times magazine, 9.8.2003

There is a more comprehensive list of reference articles on www.vernoncoleman.com

Printed in Great Britain
by Amazon

268270b0-4dbb-4d8e-8def-0958bfefa3b3R01